THE FLEET'S IN

HOLLYWOOD PRESENTS
THE U.S. NAVY IN WORLD WAR II

BY HARVEY BEIGEL

Even the movie *This Is The Army*, 1943, saluted the Navy in this scene entitled "How about a cheer for the Navy."
COURTESY OF THE ACADEMY OF MOTION PICTURE ARTS AND SCIENCES

PICTORIAL HISTORIES PUBLISHING COMPANY, INC.

LIBRARY OF CONGRESS
CATALOG CARD NO. 94-67574

ISBN 0-929521-91-9

First Printing: August 1994

Layout: Stan Cohen
Typography: Arrow Graphics
Cover Graphics: Mike Egeler

PICTORIAL HISTORIES PUBLISHING CO., INC.
713 South Third Street West, Missoula, Montana 59801

PREFACE

The Los Angeles area is the ideal place for doing research on motion pictures and the motion picture industry. Busy with productions underway, the motion picture studios may not be able to help the researcher. But they have in the last few years moved many of their records to several libraries and archives in and around the City. The most comprehensive collection of data on motion pictures is to be found at the Margaret Herrick Library in Beverly Hills. Run by the Academy of Motion Picture Arts and Sciences, this facility has files on most of the films made in Hollywood. These collections include scripts, production papers and correspondence, reviews, and relevant news article from around the country. It has a vast collection of monographs and biographies and is a valuable repository for stills. Trade papers and important documents are also held there. The author wishes to thank the many people at the Herrick Library who graciously helped him. Another repository of film material is the Warner Bros. Archives, located on the campus of the University of Southern California (USC) where material about Warner Bros. pictures can be found in abundance. This includes scripts, production papers, inter-studio communications and correspondence, reviews, stills and musical scores. Leith Adams and Stuart Ng were of great help to the author in bringing Warner Bros. files to the USC campus. Like the Margaret Herrick Library, the film library at USC has a large collection of monographs, biographies and trade publications. The Universisty of California at Los Angeles (UCLA) is a repository for Twentieth Century Fox studios; many rare films can be found in its archives located in Hollywood.

In research of this kind, the film itself is a primary source and must be seen and studied. Fortunately, many of the movies can be rented in video stores. Hard to find films can be found at the Library of Congress Film Library in Washington D.C. and the UCLA Film Archives. The best stocked video store in the area is Eddie Brandt's Saturday Matinee in North Hollywood. Stills and posters are available in several stores in the Los Angeles area. Among the most complete stores are Larry Edmund's in Hollywood and Eddie Brandt's.

Finally, the author wishes to express his thanks to his wife, Elizabeth Buchanan Beigel, whose patience, encouragment, suggestions and editing skill helped make this book possible. Moreover, the very idea for the subject of this book was hers. The author also wishes to express his thanks to Richard B. Beigel for his computer expertise which facilitated the production of the book.

ABOUT THE AUTHOR

Harvey M. Beigel, author of *The Fleet's In: Hollywood Presents the U.S. Navy in World War II*, retired in 1991 after serving 35 years in the Los Angeles Unified School District. As a history teacher at Venice High School, he served as Department Chairman of Social Studies and as a consultant for the College Board's Advanced Placement program. Mr. Beigel served in the United States Air Force during the Korean War. His first book, *Battleship Country: The Battle Fleet at San Pedro-Long Beach, California–1919-1940*, was published in 1983. He has also published a number of articles, mainly about naval history, in the Naval Institute's *Proceedings, Sea Classics* magazine, *Warship International* and *Alert*, the official publication of the Fort Mac Arthur Military Museum, located in San Pedro, California. He resides with his wife, Elizabeth, in Rancho Palos Verdes, California.

TABLE OF CONTENTS

1

BACKGROUND

After the First World War, interest in films about the military services waned because of a nationwide revulsion against violence and war. By the mid-twenties, however, this attitude began to change as a number of these motion pictures became popular again. *The Big Parade* (1925) and *Wings* (1927) depicted combat and brought out large crowds. There were very few pictures about the Navy at this time because the American naval experience in the war was limited and relatively un-dramatic. Motion picture companies were not inspired by stories about convoy duty or the work of the American battle fleet in the North Sea. Yet stories about the ships and planes of the U.S. Navy did provide opportunities to produce some romantic, comic, and dramatic pictures of a non-combat nature a full decade before World War II broke out. These films were both popular and profitable mainly because the public was interested in ships, aircraft, the sea, and sailors. This was especially true for those Americans who lived inland and craved action and adventure. In the early thirties, Hollywood brought to the screen two very popular films about the Navy. They were John Ford's silent film *Men Without Women* (1930) which introduced Americans to the lurid Shanghai waterfront and the innards of a dying submarine and Frank W. Wead's *Hell Divers* (1931) which graphically portrayed naval airmen in training aboard an aircraft carrier and their travels to exotic places.

The Navy used motion pictures to inform the public about what it was doing and how it was spending taxpayers' dollars for defense. In an age of isolationism and pacifism the Navy was very sensitive to calls for budget cuts that it thought would threaten America's security. In order to get the Navy's point of view over to the public, it created a Public Relations Office to deal with the media and put it directly under the office of Chief of Naval Operations. It was felt that a favorably impressed citizenry would press Congress to pass the needed legislation for a strong Navy. Lloyd Bacon, a director of films about the Navy, wrote that movies "are the best link with the public in inland counties and landlocked communities."[1]

It was therefore necessary that the naval service create an image that would please the American people. Motion pictures were ideally suited for this task because they were seen by wide audiences and popular charismatic actors often times played roles as naval characters. The Navy's aims could be achieved by showing them as men of virtue, honor, patriotism with "Don't give up the ship" heroics. Even if a movie character fell short of these ideals, he could still redeem himself before the end of the picture. For example, heroic action in the movie *Submarine Patrol* (1938) by a character played by Preston Foster allowed this officer to wipe clean the mistake he had made in losing a former command.

The film *Shipmates Forever* (1935) portrays the proper image of a naval officer. In the script, Admiral Melville (Lewis Stone) the retiring commander of the Battle Fleet, was thus described as a man who had the "bearing the service and tradition had given him." He told his son who refused to go to the Naval Academy that "your forbearers have always served country and flag . . . not dollars." The admiral's parting words as he gave up his command were "keep the fleet fit to fight." And even his recalcitrant son finally admits what a great institution the Navy is when he sings the title song which says the same thing musically and a bit more lightheartedly:

SHIPMATES FOREVER

Don't give up the ship
Shipmates stand together
Don't give up the ship
Fair or stormy weather
We won't give up, we won't give
Up the ship
Friends and pals forever
It's a long, long trip
If you have to take a
Licken'
Carry on and quit your kicken'
Don't give up the ship[2]

Screenwriter Michael Fessier put forth ideals that the

---

1. Memo from Robert S. Taplinger to George K. Schaffer. November 18, 1938. Production file, "Wings of the Navy." Warner Bros. Archives. U.S.C.

2. Production File, *Shipmates Forever.* Warner Bros. Archives. U.S.C.

Navy and its supporters wanted to share with the American public in the 1938 script for Warner Bros'. *Wings of the Navy*. In a note to the movie's producer, he focused on the picture's theme when he described what younger brother Jerry (John Payne) has to do to out do his older brother Cass (George Brent) as a naval aviator. "He would have to understand that interdependency of one to the whole is more than individual brilliance." "And that greatness can only come when you obey the rules."[3]

Because the motion picture was such a powerful force in arousing public interest, the Navy was careful to protect its image. The only knowledge about the Navy most Americans got was from the screen. To keep its good name, the Navy insisted on scripts that treated the Navy in a positive way. To defend itself, it would withhold cooperation from the moviemakers. This would deny the film company the use of ships and other equipment and the studio would have to settle for using model ships and planes. The credibility of the entire movie would therefore be at risk.

In 1932, Chief of Naval Operations William V. Pratt clearly spelled out conditions motion picture companies would have to agree to before the Navy would offer their resources for a film. First, the studio would have to send a script with a request for cooperation with a statement of the nature of the required cooperation. No scripts about foreign navies would be accepted, nor could American vessels be shown with a flag of another country. American naval personnel could not impersonate members of a foreign navy in the film story. The picture could not contain anything that might bring discredit to any branch of the American government or any foreign government service or the personnel or uniform of such service.[4] Most important, the motion picture could not contain any offense to public morals or good taste, a large order for film studios whose profits were derived from pictures based on exaggeration and overstatement. In a revised statement, the Navy indicated that it would not countenance any movie which gave the "public a false impression of the moral discipline and conduct of the personnel of the Navy." The Navy insisted that cooperation must not interfere with normal fleet operations. When the film was completed, it had to be reviewed by the Navy's Motion Picture Film Board and approved. The Board consisted of a recruiting officer, a morale officer, a public relations officer, and a censorship officer, all working under the Chief of Naval Operations.

Other conditions placed on the studios by the Motion Picture Film Board were: Navy personnel in a film could not be used in any hazardous undertaking and that Navy equipment would not be subject to undue risk. Strict rules in the making of photographs were to be adhered to as well.

Officers detailed as Technical Supervisors were authorized to censor on the spot any scene violating the rules and conditions attached to naval cooperation. The film company would have to assume all financial liability for the death or injury or the loss of property resulting from the production of the picture. No compensation would be paid to naval personnel other than reimbursement for actual expense, injury or loss of property. The Navy Department was to be given free of charge two final prints of the approved picture. Finally, if the production involved outlays beyond normal fleet operations, the producer was required to make a special deposit covering the estimated cost.

Many of the sea movies of the 1930s did not receive a naval seal of approval for cooperation and were cancelled; other films were modified and finally approved. One officer working under the Chief of Naval Operations praised American film companies for making foreign service films with extreme care. He, however, had little to say that was good about the script of *Murder in the Fleet* which he saw as making a travesty of the American Navy by showing women running around on a battleship. In 1938, Acting CNO Admiral James O. Richardson turned down the Universal Picture *The Black Fleet* for having technical errors and violations of naval regulations and customs. Not only did the film show misleading perceptions of naval activities, its theme dealt with both espionage and complications with foreign governments. Therefore cooperation was denied this picture, and the film company was prevented from using stock scenes made available by other movie studios.[5] MGM's *Born Dancing* (Formerly *Great Guns*) was approved by the Navy in 1936, but on the condition that references to oriental spies, the using of Japanese names, and the belittling of New Deal expenditures be deleted. The Columbia Pictures' script *Heroes Come High* was so objectionable and harmful to the Navy's interests, it did not receive an official critique from the Navy Department.

Ever sensitive to the stereotype of the "Drunken Sailor," Navy officials were careful to check scripts which portrayed sailors unfavorably. If RKO producer Pandro Berman wanted naval cooperation for his picture *Follow the Fleet*, he would have to delete any suggestive female talk, a scene showing drunken sailors fighting, and another

3. Inter-office Communication to Lou Edelman from Michael Fessier. January 7, 1938. Production File, *Wings of the Navy*. Warner Bros. Archives. U.S.C.

4. *Policy of the Navy Department Concerning Cooperation in the Production of Commercial Motion Picture Plays.* 5 August 1932.

5. Letter to Irene Muto of the Motion Picture Producers and Distributors of America, Inc., from Admiral J. O. Richardson, Acting CNO, April 29, 1938. National Archives, Record Group 80. Box 419.

SHIPMATES, 1932

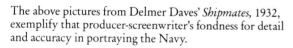

The above pictures from Delmer Daves' *Shipmates*, 1932, exemplify that producer-screenwriter's fondness for detail and accuracy in portraying the Navy.

Top Left: A ship's captain looks out at the San Pedro Fleet anchorage with a Maryland-class battleship and the Palos Verdes Peninsula in the background.

Top Right: Naval gunnery.

Bottom Left: A sailor played by Robert Montgomery readies himself for liberty.

Bottom Right: Montgomery leaves the fleet for Annapolis, where he meets his sweetheart played by Dorothy Jordan.

showing wine being served in the Navy. A drinking scene in the movie *The Blue and the Gold* was deleted for the same reason. While the film was ok'd for release in November 1937, a Naval Academy official wrote that the film was still "not that good."[6] The Navy was even particular about who played the roles of Navy personnel on the screen. For example, they did not want the studios to hire actors who had been cast as crooks or drunks in their previous roles. For that reason, some of Hollywood's best character actors, even those with spotless private lives, could never get a role commanding a battleship or any other kind of ship for that matter. There was, however, one exception and that was Frank McHugh, the star of such hits as *Here Comes the Navy*, *Devil Dogs of the Air*, and *Submarine D-1*. In McHugh's case, he was considered so amiable "even when potted," that "he did not offend the Navy's sensitivities."[7]

The question of security could occasionally cause the Navy to not cooperate with a studio in the production of a navy topic. Security matters were becoming the subject of growing concern as tension with Japan in the mid-thirties increased. Not only did Admiral Joseph M. Reeves CINCUS (Commander and Chief of the United States Fleet) put the fleet then massed in California on alert for a possible sneak attack, he also clamped down on allowing security leaks seen in films that might hurt the Navy. In 1935, Warner Bros. asked for naval cooperation in the making of a submarine movie it called *Submarine 262* and later changed to *Submarine D-1*. Reeves opposed the making of the picture not only for its probable interference with the submarine force's work schedule, but because scenes of the submarine's interiors might compromise naval security. He flatly opposed cooperation because he knew that Navy rules prohibited photographing a United States submarine underway. The author of the film's screenplay Frank W. Wead, a former naval officer, saw a way around this security problem. His idea was that all necessary exterior scenes with the cast aboard could be shot while the sub was anchored or moored along its depot ship. While the submarine was cruising, the crew could be grouped in such a way that close shots of the actors could easily be made later in the studio. As far as the interior shots were concerned, Wead believed that by using official sketches, authentic submarine interiors could be made on the studio's back lot without compromising security.[8]

In December 1936, Warner Bros. received word that the Chief of Naval Operations had approved the film and ordered that submarine bases extend their cooperation. The picture was finally approved because the Review Board liked the script and security fears were calmed. It seemed that the withholding of some of the secret or

Fleet commander Joseph M. Reeves made it difficult for Hollywood to make films about the Navy. NATIONAL ARCHIVES

confidential information would not be crucial for the success of the movie. Finally, Admiral Reeves left the fleet and no longer could impede the film's progress. Warner Bros. film *Submarine D-1* was previewed in Hollywood on November 8, 1937. Footage was shot at Panama, New London, and San Diego and was sent back to Washington D.C. as a security request of Admiral James O. Richardson, Deputy CNO.[9]

Hollywood movies played a key role in Navy recruitment campaigns. Though the number of recruits was scaled down in the early thirties, it was expanded later in the decade. Particularly sought after were recruits with technical knowledge. It was hoped that the appeal of adventure, romance, and travel could wean skilled men away from their civilian jobs. It was because this program did not attract enough skilled men, that the Navy began to increase the number of its own technical schools.

An excellent working relationship between Warner Bros. Productions and the Navy took place during this

6. Memo, Comdr. V. J. Larson, Aide to Superintendent Naval Academy, 22 July 1937. National Archives Record Group 80, Box 423.

7. "The Navy Casts Hollywood Films." Warner Bros. publicity Department, Vol. I, No. 26, n.d., Production File, *Wings of the Navy*, Warner Bros. Archives, U.S.C.

8. Letter to Captain Paul Bastedo, Office of the CNO, from Frank W. Wead, November 22, 1935. Production File, "Submarine D-1," Warner Bros. Archives. U.S.C.

9. Letter from H. J. McCord to J. I. Warner, January 11, 1938. *Ibid.*

The ever-popular movie *Here Comes the Navy*, 1934, was re-released just before the U.S. entered World War II. Here James Cagney readies a large battleship rifle.

period. Screenwriter Frank W. Wead and Director Lloyd Bacon were both on the Warner payroll and were former naval officers. They both understood the problems of production and the requirements of the Navy. With the success of so many of Warner's Navy films and the call for a larger Navy, it was natural that cooperation between the studio and the Navy would grow. Even the 1934 movie *Here Comes the Navy* was re-released in the late '30s and early '40s to encourage interest in America's defense effort.[10] Warner's Lloyd Bacon believed that Hollywood motion pictures provided the best "medium" through which schoolboys obtain their ideas about what national service is, "and that these films go a long way to solve the problem of manning the fleet." High ranking naval officials believed that Warner's forthcoming production *Wings of the Navy*, (1939) would inspire a "high type of individual" to enter naval flight training. Marc A. Mitcher of the Navy's Bureau of Aeronautics praised the succeeding Warner production *Dive Bomber*, (1941) because it would "... advertise the Aviation Cadet Program and that is what we're interested in at the present time."[11]

When the movie *Dive Bomber* was released in the Spring of 1941, an accommodating Warner Bros. asked its distributors and theater owners to allow naval displays in their lobbies in conjunction with the film. Eye and reflex tests were also set up to measure movie patrons' fitness for naval service. Most impressive was the Navy's agreement with the studio to advertise *Dive Bomber* by placing Navy planes on exhibition in principal American cities. The showings were in Los Angeles, California, at Pershing Square and in New York City at Times Square. Recruiting booths were set up and real dive bombers were placed nearby to both advertise joining the fleet and to get the attention of the general public as well.[12] This type of promotion was not new for Warner Bros. Battleship floats manned by "Girl Sailors" were parked outside movie houses to publicize *Here Comes the Navy* (1934); theaters showing *Submarine D-1* (1937) also featured a float with "Girl Sailors," this time riding abreast of a powerful submarine.

As movie productions began to present the armed services in a more favorable light, pacifist and isolationist groups began to show their ire. While anti-war pictures had not grown in popularity since the great success of *All Quiet on the Western Front* (1930), many of the newer films tended to romanticize military life and naval service. Some of these groups argued that military cooperation with the studios was a form of government subsidization of the motion picture industry and that the taxpayer had to pay twice to see a movie, once with taxes and once at the box office. One Illinois constituent wrote his senator that the government ought to make Warner Bros. pay $25,000 for the help it got from the Navy in filming *Submarine D-1*. The situation was so explosive that Secretary of the Navy Clause Swanson warned pro-Navy legislators that this argument would be used against adding money to naval build-up. In a scathing attack on the proliferation of service films, the *Christian Century*, an

10. John Davis, "Notes on Warner Brothers Foreign Policy, 1919–1948," *The Velvet Light Trap of Cinema*, No. 4, Spring, 1972, p. 25.

11. Letter to Frank W. Wead from "Pete" Mitscher, Bureau of Aeronautics, Navy Department. October 24, 1940. Production File, *Dive Bomber*. Warner Bros. Archives, U.S.C.

12. Press Book, *Dive Bomber*, Warner Bros. Archives. U.S.C.

anti-war periodical, asserted that the Army and Navy were keeping pacifist themes out of the movies by withholding federal aid (Army or Navy cooperation) from these kinds of films. For example, they said that the logical anti-war conclusion in the motion picture *Men With Wings* was eliminated because it had a "tinge of what may be regarded as pacifist doctrine." Moreover, they said that motion pictures companies were preparing Americans for war. They cited *Submarine D-1*, *Wings of the Navy*, *Navy Blue and Gold*, *Submarine Patrol*, and the *Duke of West Point* as blatant examples of this.[13]

By 1941, an isolationist non-interventionist backlash grew in intensity as the United States moved close to full participation in the war against Nazi Germany. Disturbed because of the growth of pro-war feeling, isolationist senators sought any means to stop this drift. They told the American people that they were being duped into believing that further intervention was necessary by both the Roosevelt Administration and war propaganda disseminated by the motion picture industry. On September 9, 1941, the isolationist-dominated Senate Committee on Interstate Commerce began hearings to investigate propaganda in Hollywood films. They wanted to balance these films with others that gave another side to the story about intervention in the European War. Some opponents immediately retorted that the isolationists were doing this because they were losing the foreign policy debate with the American people, while Wendell Willkie, the motion picture industry's leading defense attorney, said the investigation was strictly a publicity stunt.[14]

Although the main thrust of the hearings was to show that anti-Nazi films like the *Great Dictator* and *Confessions of a Nazi Spy* were being produced by a "Hollywood, Anglo, Jewish" cabal to get the United States to fight, it also included a list of recently released service films. Though these films carried little explicit propaganda, they were perceived by anti-war activists as being pro-war because they all praised the armed services.

Harry Warner, responding to the anti-Semitic tenor of the hearings, said while he would not deny that he was anti-Nazi (as most Americans were), that did not mean that Warner Bros. productions were propagandistic. Nicholas Schenk, President of Loews, the parent company of Metro-Golden-Mayer studios, defended MGM's *Flight Command* by declaring to the Committee that it was a picture "that had nothing to do with anybody with the exception of a love story."[15] Willkie characterized his Hollywood clients as patriotic Americans who had done everything they could to present to the American people "picture(s) of our Army, our Navy, and Air Corps, and their equipment." He also told the Committee that a "person's racial or geographic background should not be a

reason for this investigation."[16]

Some of the Committee members bungled their own investigation by lacking familiarity with the films they were reviewing. For example, Gerald P. Nye of North Dakota, a leading member of the Committee and an ardent isolationist, confused the title of the film *I Married a Nazi* with *Confessions of a Nazi Spy*. Robert Champ Clark of Missouri called Warner Bros. the greatest producer of hate films in America and told a colleague that he had not seen one film being discussed and intended never to see them. But Senator Charles Tobey of New Hampshire told the Committee that he could not see how the movie *Dive Bomber* could be construed as propaganda, but chided Hollywood for using members of the armed forces as actors in these films.[17]

By October, the Committee was still unable to find any incriminating evidence that there was an interventionist conspiracy in the movie industry. Meanwhile, the Committee was losing the support of the moderate wing of the isolationist movement. The Committee recessed on September 21, 1941, and did not reconvene after the Japanese attack on Pearl Harbor on December 7, 1941. So much for the Senate Hearings. A leading interventionist group characterized the efforts of the Committee as a "barefooted attempt at censorship and racial prejudice."[18]

13. "Liberty Bells in Hollywood." *Christian Century*, March 8, 1939, p. 310.

14. *Time*, September 22, 1941.

15. U.S. Congress. Senate, Committee on Interstate Commerce, Propaganda in Motion Pictures, Hearings before a sub-committee of the Senate Committee on Interstate Commerce, 77th Congress, September 1941, p. 333.

16. *Ibid.*, p. 19.

17. *Ibid.*, p. 355.

18. *Newsweek*, September 15, 1941. p. 52.

A battlefleet commander, portrayed by Lewis Stone, talks to his son, played by Dick Powell, on the deck of his flagship in *Shipmates Forever*, 1935.

2

GETTING IN A FIGHTING MOOD
Peacetime War Movies, 1938-1941

While combat films like *All Quiet on the Western Front* did not appear in any appreciable number in the 1930s, peacetime military films emphasizing adventure, romance, travel, and patriotic symbolism did. However, this pattern of movie-making began to break down as a result of Hitler's seizure of Austria and Czechoslovakia in 1938 and the outbreak of World War II in 1939. Because of the high-level of interest in the war in the United States, studios began to look for scripts which depicted the reality of war. Two of the first films produced to meet this demand were about American sub-chasers during the First World War. These small craft were the Navy's stars during the war and U-Boats had an historical fascination in the United States. *Submarine Patrol* (1938) and *Thunder Afloat* (1939) both pitted Americans against Germans. Though the sailors aboard the U-Boats in these pictures were not Nazis, the fact that they were Germans was enough to rekindle the anti-Germanism of the previous war. The Academy Award winning *Sergeant York* released in 1941 was the most successful of this kind of film.

Love takes hold between Richard Greene and Nancy Kelly in *Submarine Patrol*.

SUBMARINE PATROL

Submarine Patrol was released at the height of the Munich Crisis on November 25, 1938. The picture was taken from the non-fiction material in Ray Millholland's book *The Splinter Fleet of the Otranto Barrage*. The film's title was *The Splinter Fleet*, later changed to *Wooden Anchors*. The title *Submarine Patrol* was finally chosen because it focused the public's attention on the frightening undersea warfare that had already taken place and might do so again.

This action movie is about the heroic crew of a small, but daring sub-chaser during the First World War. The Navy provided the studio with real sub-chasers to enhance the film's authenticity. The picture's two main characters are Perry Townsend III (Richard Greene)

whose family connections and yachting experience win him an immediate Chief Petty Officer rating and Lt. (J.G.) John C. Drake (Robert Preston) whose carelessness in a prior destroyer grounding put his career under a cloud of suspicion. The rest of the crew is comedic, good-natured, but poorly trained. Discipline aboard the ship is nowhere to be found. The cook played by Slim Summerfield actually runs his own restaurant on the side and one of his ship-mates drives a cab when not on duty. On board, there is also a young man known as the "Professor." He keeps guinea pigs which the crew fears will wind up in the cook's stew. After a small contingent of regular

Navy men appear, the crew is trained and the sub-chaser becomes ready for action. The film also features a love story between Townsend and the daughter of a merchant ship captain Susan Leeds (Nancy Kelly). They meet on the dock and it is love at first sight. But there are complications. Her father does not believe this rich man is sincere and wants the romance to end. He even has a scuffle with Townsend. The ship carrying Susan and her father and the sub-chaser are ordered to Italy. The romance continues and the ship captain finally realizes Townsend's good intentions.

The climax of the story is when the sub-chaser is sent up the coast to destroy the famous German raider "Ole 26." Drake is ready for action and leads his crew on what appears to be a suicide mission. Instead, he miraculously sinks the enemy craft and destroys its base of operations as well.

The movie does make a number of interesting points. First, it shows that a man of privilege must adjust to the fact that he is no better than the average sailor in time of war. In the case of Drake, it shows that a man can redeem himself from the taint of earlier mistakes if he persists and does not give up. Lastly, the story points out that while Americans come from different ethnic backgrounds, they can pull together in adversity and face the enemy with daring and courage.

A humorous post-script to this film is the unusual amount of accidents that befell the cast during the filming of the movie. The worst mishap was when actor Elisha Cook Jr. lost an inch of his thumb when he caught it on a wire during a storm scene. Richard Greene just missed being hit by a studio light which had plummeted 20 feet to the ground. After being hit by a ball, director John Ford ordered him to quit playing baseball on the lot. Greene also hurt his thumb when some fireworks exploded on the Fourth of July. Then a stand-in for Preston Poster cracked his knee and partially paralyzed his left leg when he slipped and fell between two sub-chasers moored in a tank on the sound stage. To add to all this confusion, an "extra" was badly bruised when he fell during a mad scramble on the deck of a German submarine.[1]

THUNDER AFLOAT

The exploits of another American sub-chaser in the First World War was the subject of the Metro-Goldwyn-Mayer's *Thunder Afloat* which entered production on May 23, 1939. Like Fox's *Submarine Patrol*, the film showed the Navy dealing with the same enemy, the mysterious German U-Boat. The film was completed on July 12, 1939, but was not released until a few weeks after

Europe had plunged into World War II on September 1, 1939. The Roosevelt Administration wanted to delay its showing in order to stimulate interest in the ongoing debate on rearmament.[2] MGM acquiest to the government's request and held back the film's release until September 24. In an attempt to exploit the public's interest in the outbreak of war, the studio suggested that movie houses either set up a float of a sub-chaser or a submarine in front of their box-offices. They advised movie managers that the submarine "crews" on the float wear simple German wartime uniforms!

Thunder Afloat is yet another story about the heroic exploits of American sub-chasers during World War I. The film opens in a New England fishing port where Navy recruiters come to enlist experienced men, especially local skippers. They need men to man the over five hundred sub-chasers built during the war. Tug boat Captain Thorson (Wallace Berry) has just been cheated out of a contract by rival, Rocky Blake (Chester Morris). He has smashed the valves in Thorson's boat. Susan (Virginia Grey) gets an idea on how to trick Rocky and win back the lost contract. She flirts and convinces him to be patriotic and join the Navy. Her father, who has called Rocky "yellow" feels compelled to join the Navy himself. Rocky enlists, but Thorson backs out after he decides he can do financially better with his tug boat. But when Thorson's boat is mined by a German U-Boat, anger takes over and he joins the Navy with a commission and command of a sub-chaser. Meanwhile the romance between Susan and Blake heats up and he tells her he holds no grudge against her father. When Thorson attempts to capture a U-Boat and fails, he is reprimanded by Blake, now a division commander and busted to the rank of regular seaman. As submarine warfare grows in intensity, the navy fits out the Glouchester schooner *Phinnie G.* as an anti-submarine decoy ship. Thorson, a member of the crew, leaves the schooner on a dory to do his own thing, but instead is captured by the enemy raider. Heroically, he gives away the U-Boats position by banging on its hull and the sub-chasers capture the U-Boat. Blake and Susan are happily reunited and Thorson is given back his commission. Thorson is the ultimate individualist and proves it under fire. In the final analysis, however, he finds out that the Navy is bigger than any one skipper. The picture shows that the Germans are deceitful in sinking small ships and will eventually lose the war.

1. Production file, *Submarine Patrol*, Academy of Motion Picture Arts and Sciences. Margaret Herrick Library. Beverly Hills, CA.

2. Michael T. Isenberg. *War on Films: The American Cinema in World War I. 1914–1941.* (London and Toronto: Farleigh Dickinson Press, 1981). p. 117.

An individualist at heart, Wallace Beery learns to become a team player and helps capture a German U-boat.

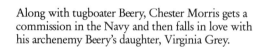Along with tugboater Beery, Chester Morris gets a commission in the Navy and then falls in love with his archenemy Beery's daughter, Virginia Grey.

German U-boat captains are not to be trusted by innocent seamen.

The Navy extended full cooperation in the making of *Thunder Afloat*. It still had twelve sub-chasers on the east coast when the film was being made. Six of them were reconditioned with parts collected from naval warehouses and ordinance yards around the country. Most the film's exterior scenes were filmed from the submarine *USS Sturgeon* (SS-187) off Coronado, California. To complete the film, the studio built three of its own sub-chasers and placed them in an outdoor tank. Another one was built and placed in a second tank. These small ships were built complete with Y-guns and depth charges, but they had shell-like hulls. Buildings and landings of a New England port were also built by studio craftsman. The *Glouchester* schooner was built specifically for MGM in Long Beach, California. The U-Boat interiors were constructed in sections with the aid of a German advisor.[3]

Though made 20 years after the end of World War I, this scene from *Thunder Afloat* is sure to rekindle anti-German feelings. Beery is captured by a U-boat crew.

WINGS OF THE NAVY

Franklin D. Roosevelt's call for a naval buildup in January, 1938 was denounced by historian Charles A. Beard in his book *America at Midpassage*. In it, he specifically charged that Warner Bros.' *Wings of the Navy* was a propagandistic picture created to further FDR's foreign policy goals. Beard also stated in the *New York*

Times that it was government pressure that had squelched pacifist preachments in another film.[4] Warner Bros. was given close cooperation from the Navy. The important air facilities at Pensacola, Florida and North Island, California were open to the film company. *Wings of the Navy* would certainly tell the public in some detail how their money was being spent by the Navy.

The close connection between the government and the studios which Beard lamented can also be seen in a studio memo written to producer Hal Wallis on November 1, 1938. It states that "The picture [*Wings of the Navy*] certainly advocates the President's policy." Moreover a presidential quote on the film's trailer has FDR saying that "we must be prepared to meet with success any application of force against us."[5] The viewing of many of the Navy's most advanced planes in one sequence was sure to lend credibility to the president's statement both at home and abroad.

Wings of the Navy released on January 11, 1939 begins with the two naval officers unveiling a monument in Arlington, Virginia. The ceremony commemorates the self-sacrifice and inspiration that the pioneer Admiral Harrington had given to his country. The young men are his sons, Cass (George Brent), one of the country's great airmen and his younger brother Jerry (John Payne), an ensign in the submarine service.

Jerry is so impressed by the tribute to his father that he leaves the submarine service for one in aviation. In training, Jerry, like so many others, has a difficult time meeting the high standards of flight school. He meets his brother's warm-hearted and vivacious fiancee Irene Dale (Olivia de Haviland) and both are immediately drawn to each other.

During flight training at Pensacola, Jerry, always trying to live up to his father and his brother (who is developing a new type of fighter aircraft), almost washes out. He is fortunate to have a cool and efficient flight instructor Lt. White (John Gallaudet), and so he survives. There is comic relief in the picture with cadet "Scat" Allen (Frank McHugh). Allen, who comes to the Navy from Iowa State Agriculture College and really wants to fly in order to spray potato bugs from the air, turns out to be an excellent airman.

When Cass Harrington goes to Washington D.C. to discuss the plans for a new Navy fighter plane, he leaves his brother to escort Irene. Both soon realize that they are in love. Upon his return, Cass mistakes his younger brother's moodiness for "puppy love." Loyal to his brother,

3. Production File, *Thunder Afloat*. Academy of Motion Picture Arts and Sciences, Margaret Herrick Library, Beverly Hills, CA.

4. *New York Times*, May 28, 1938.

5. Press Book, Preview Section. *Wings of the Navy*. Warner Bros. Archives. U.S.C.

There is plenty of activity at North Island Naval Air Station as a Warner Bros. production crew film several squadrons of Consolidated PBY-2 *Catalina* patrol bombers. © 1939 TURNER ENTERTAINMENT CO.

Jerry urges Irene not to break her engagement with Cass, after the older brother is almost killed in a serious air crash and is forced to leave the Navy.

Ordered to Naval Air Station (NAS) North Island, Jerry receives further training in the new PBY-2 flying boat. Jerry's fortunes seem better than his brother's when his PBY-2 "Flying Destroyer" bombs and destroys a derelict ammunition ship which is endangering coastal shipping. On the other hand, Cass hears that his projected fighter plane has crashed and killed the pilot. Jerry then resigns his commission to test another model of Cass's plane. The tests prove successful and Cass's plane is accepted. Jerry is reinstated in the Navy and is ordered to fly one of the PBY-2 planes from San Diego to Hawaii.

Proud of his kid brother, Cass makes Jerry's decision

to return to the Navy easier by releasing his fiancee from their engagement. A strong thread in the story is the deep loyalty and affection the brothers have for each other. Present throughout the film and restated often are naval-air innovations. An example of this is the colossal nature of the new PBY-2 which can span huge distances in the Pacific Ocean. The film's messages are cleverly interspersed between the love and personal stories to keep the audience amused and interested. The film was popular with both the critics and the public.

Wings of the Navy cost $1,000,000 to produce, an enormous sum at the time. The huge cast and technical crew worked at two locations, NAS Pensacola in Florida and NAS North Island near San Diego. It took nine weeks to shoot the picture, with one-third of the time spent

The Harrington brothers, John Payne (left) and George Brent (right), both naval aviators, confront each other in *Wings of the Navy*, 1939.

at the studio. Many of the flying sequences were made in Pensacola. It was against Navy regulations for its men to receive renumerations for flying for commercial gain, so Lt. E.R. Miller flew for free because of his own sense of fun and a love of flying. Civilians Paul Mantz and Frank Clarke flew the more dangerous maneuvers like a plane falling into a dangerous spin, a stunt not allowed by the Navy. All the film's photography was done by Mantz in his camera ship.[6]

Warner Bros. not only worked with the Navy, but with Consolidated Aircraft Corporation of San Diego, the makers of the PBY-2 *Catalina* patrol bomber. The company lent the studio pilot seats, instrument panels, and other equipment. Most importantly, they helped studio technicians build a full-scale model of the flying boat which was used for close-up shots of the big plane in flight. One naval aviator visiting the studio was so impressed by the replica of the plane that he jokingly told people on the set that all the *Catalina* needed was gasoline and he'd "take it right through your sound stage roof."[7]

FLIGHT COMMAND

MGM's *Flight Command* released in January 1941 is yet another film dedicated to the naval air service. It was made with the full cooperation of the Navy Department which desperately needed pilots. With the European war in its second year and the defeat of France a fact, the movie is more involved with the war than its Warner Bros.' predecessor. Talk about the heroism of a British pilot at Dunkirk and the fact that the U.S. Navy "is the first

line of defense when the chips are down" are subjects talked about by the carrier pilots in training. The immediacy of the war is ever present in this film.

Flight Command is about a young "know it all" Ensign Alan Drake (Robert Taylor). Ordered to a crack West Coast fighter squadron VF-8, the famed "Hellcats," Drake is elated because he believes he is their choice from among the graduating class of Pensacola. Unfortunately, this is not the case and he soon learns that his shipmates feel the squadron is too tough for a "cadet." Only the squadron Skipper (Walter Pidgeon) makes him feel at home. During machine gun target practice, he tries too hard and runs into the target, thereby putting the squadron out of the competition with other units. The other flyers "chill" him and if that is not enough, they let him know that he was not specifically chosen to fly with the "Hellcats." The scarcity of pilots due to the National Defense Program buildup now sends graduating cadets to wherever they are needed and that includes the "Hellcats." Some of the flyers open up to Drake at a party given by the skipper's wife Lorna (Ruth Hussy) and he is on the road to acceptance.

Drake then befriends Lorna's brother Lt. Jerry Banning (Sheppard Strudwick) who is working on an anti-fog device. After Jerry is tragically killed in a crash, Drake decides to continue the project. He is asked to resign from the squadron when he is falsely accused of romancing the skipper's wife Lorna. But before his resignation becomes final, he has to accompany the squadron on maneuvers. The skipper is forced to crash-land his plane

6. Don Dwiggens, *Hollywood Pilot: The Biography of Paul Mantz* (Garden City: Doubleday, 1967), p. 68.

7. Harold Turney, *Film Guide to Wings of the Navy* (Los Angeles City College, 1938), p. 5.

Promotional picture of leading players—Ruth Hussy, Robert Taylor and Walter Pidgeon—in the MGM epic *Flight Command*, 1941. It was VF-6 at North Island that portrayed fictional VF-8.

after it springs a leak. Going against orders, Drake follows the skipper down, finds him, and takes him aboard his small F-3F-2 fighter plane. Since Drake is carrying Jerry's instrument landings device, he is able to land the plane safely in the heavy fog, and he leads in the other "Hellcats." When the pilots see that Drake has saved the skipper and that he is blameless in the affair with Lorna, the squadron refuses to let him resign.

Preparations for the film began in early 1940. Knowing that naval cooperation was absolutely essential for the picture's success, Producer J. Walter Ruben worked for months with his screenwriters to make the project acceptable to the Navy. At first, the script was rejected because it was thought that the dialogue was too tough. The writers went to work and the studio got the green light when they modified the script. The selection of Walter Pidgeon and Robert Taylor pleased the Navy.

In June 1940, the producer Ruben brought the film company down to NAS North Island where work began on the film. They were met there by the aviators of VF-6, a crack fighter squadron. For two weeks their small but sturdy F-3F-2s were tracked by director Frank Borage

and his cameras. Paul Mantz ably assisted by stunt pilot Frank Clarke and aviatrix Laura Ingalls did all the air-to-air photography. The problem of a missing plane in the mass formation of the entire squadron was solved later in the studio by synchronizing a second sound stage mock-up of an F-3F2 with the finished air-to-air footage. When "Fighting Six" was unexpectedly ordered to Pearl Harbor for maneuvers, the studio was given a great opportunity to film carrier operations on the USS *Enterprise* near Hawaii. Meanwhile a marine fighter group was called in to complete the last sequence that had been planned for the "Fighting Six." The proud Marines flew into San Diego, but it must have been hard for them to see their F-3F-2s being painted over with temporary Navy markings.[8]

Though the film is tied to a weak love story, it nonetheless describes the efforts of the Navy to ready its squadrons for the possibility of war. Audiences were able to view the development of fog-defying instrument landings and to witness the training of a fighter squadron.

8. Bruce V. Orriss, *When Hollywood Ruled the Skies* (Hawthorne: Aero Associates Inc., 1984), pp. 15-16.

Though flight surgeon Errol Flynn and naval aviator Fred MacMurray don't get along in Warner's *Dive Bomber*, their combined efforts will improve flight safety.

Robert Taylor tells the squadron's "exec," Paul Kelly, about his landing attempt in the fog.

Sheppard Strudwick, playing Ruth Hussy's brother, explains the workings of an experimental anti-fog device. Films of this genre stressed innovation in flight safety.

Bold scenes showing actual shots of screaming power dives, target practice, carrier takeoffs, and landings make it an impressive movie.

DIVE BOMBER

Dive Bomber, the last of so-called peacetime "war movies" was released by Warner Bros. on August 30, 1941, a little over three months before the Japanese attack on Pearl Harbor. At first, the Navy refused to cooperate in the filming of this movie because it was readying its forces for the coming conflict in the Pacific. Realizing that the film could not be made without the Navy's assistance, studio head Jack L. Warner sent one of his trusted troubleshooters Colonel William Guthrie to Washington D.C. where he discussed the matter with Secretary of the Navy Frank Knox. While it is not known whether it was the influence of the movie industry or orders from a higher political authority, the Navy did open its North Island facility and shooting began on March 20, 1941. Security was tight and normal flight operations at NAS North Island were not changed. Naval Intelligence placed stars Errol Flynn, Fred MacMurray, and Ralph Bellamy under surveillance both at the air base and the Hotel Del Coronado.[9] All members of the film company had to carry a special pass with identification numbers on them.[10]

The film *Dive Bomber* is similar to *Flight Command* in that one of its main themes is experimentation and innovation in naval flight safety. While the MGM picture concentrates on instrument flying and safety devices, *Dive Bomber* is concerned with problems which are unique to dive bombing, like pilot black-out, embolism, diving fatigue and high altitude flying. The development of pressurized cabins is also looked into.

The story begins when Lt. Douglas Lee (Errol Flynn), a Navy doctor, meets Comdr. Joe Blake (Fred MacMurray) at a naval hospital in Hawaii. A conflict between the two men begins when Lee is unable to save the life of one of Blake's buddies, an air crash victim. Lee transfers to San Diego where he can work with a leading specialist in naval medicine, Dr. Lance Rogers (Ralph Bellamy). Blake follows Lee to San Diego where he becomes a Flight Instructor at the naval air station. Blake's anger towards Lee is intensified when both men show an interest in the same woman, Linda Smith (Alexis Smith). But the problem of the love triangle disappears with little explanation as the tension between the two remains. After the flying death of another one of Joe's comrades, the aviator begins to discover the importance of Lee's work. Together

Robert Taylor tries hard to be accepted by his cohorts in a top-rated fighter squadron.

they experiment with a pressure oxygen suit that might prevent high altitude sickness. The element of distrust, however, reemerges when Lee orders Blake grounded because of chronic fatigue. Joe defies the Flight Surgeon's orders and takes his stubby F-3F-2 fighter plane aloft wearing the experimental pressure suit. At 40,000 feet Joe's oxygen is cut off when the valves and tubes of the system freeze up. Joe blacks-out and plunges to his death, but is able to leave notes that will explain what went wrong. The next day, the Naval Air Service pays tribute to a man, who in death has left information that will make flying safer for other pilots.

There are several hints in this movie that reveal that war is imminent and that England is fighting the good fight. One aviator exclaims that there are two types of black-outs, ". . . Our kind and the kind they are having in England." Another one laments the fact that a heart ailment will ground him "just as the main event is about to start." Growing Anglo-American solidarity is expressed when a former Navy pilot (Regis Toomey) brings his Royal Air Force plane in for a landing at a Navy air field. In a jovial way he asks for some gas and is told he

9. Tony Thomas, *Errol Flynn: The Spy Who Never Was* (New York: Citadel Press, 1990), p. 122.

10. Production Notes, *Dive Bomber*, Warner Bros. Archives, U.S.C.

can have it. All he has to do is sign the receipt "Winston C." and he is on his way. The American pilots are envious of their former comrade now ferrying planes to Canada for the RAF. A Navy mechanic salutes him with pride when he takes-off.[11]

Good humor was not always present in every aspect of the filming of *Dive Bomber*. Navy officials were not pleased when they heard the production company was coming aboard the USS *Enterprise* (CV-6) to film its flight operations; the carrier was conducting maneuvers off the coast of California. At first, the Navy stridently turned down the request, but a studio "fixer" got the ear of higher authorities and the film company was invited aboard.[12] While it is impossible to say whether or not the commanding officer of the *Enterprise* intentionally gave the film party a bad time, it can be said that the one week exercise offered little comfort or fun to them. They got very little sleep as the *Enterprise* conducted night battle practice daily from evening until dawn. Director Michael

Curtiz, who annoyed officers for most of the trip by pulling on their sleeves to get their attention, was horrified when billowing black smoke blocked off a badly needed close shot. Curtiz had patiently waited to do this final take as the ship prepared to dock. In his panic, he asked the captain to please blow the smoke the other way. The film people also resented the way they were rushed off the ship when it docked. Errol Flynn was very popular with everyone aboard the ship except the admiral, the captain, and those officers whose quarters were taken over by Flynn and Curtiz. An ironic footnote to Errol Flynn's presence on the aircraft carrier was that this politically anti-British actor was later accused by producer Robert Lord of being an Axis agent. This charge has never been substantiated.

11. *Dive Bomber Script, ibid.,* pp. 93-97.

12. Ralph Bellamy, *When the Smoke Hit the Fan* (New York: Doubleday & Company, 1979), p. 161.

Navy fighter pilots discuss their political views. Regis Toomey (left) decides to join the RCAF. Fred MacMurray is in the center and Louis J. Heydt is to the right. © 1941 TURNER ENTERTAINMENT CO.

Douglas TBD torpedo-bombers of VT-6 of the U.S.S. *Enterprise*'s air group participated in many scenes of *Dive Bomber*. Note the war color scheme of the planes parked at N.A.S. North Island. © 1941 TURNER ENTERTAINMENT CO.

3

GETTING IN A FIGHTING MOOD
Comedies and Musicals, 1940-1942

Along with dramatic service films, comedies and musicals gained in popularity as war clouds arose in the late 1930s. While centered around the military, the comic hero was seldom thrust into combat. The president's proclamation of an unlimited national emergency in April 1941 greatly increased the number of this type of film. By trivializing and humanizing the military experience, movies of this genre helped millions of men and their families adjust to the draft and the general mobilization for war. Moreover, worried parents might imagine from these light-hearted pictures that being in the service was not much different than going away on a youthful adventure. The main comic characters were usually misfits, outsiders, or reluctant sailors who surmounted adversity with the right amount of determination that truly reflected the American character. Along with the laughs, the movies did exhibit certain attitudes towards military life. There were authority figures like the "bullying" Sergeants or Chiefs and incompetent officers. The plot of the old 1933 comedy *Son of a Sailor* is typical of this kind of melodrama when Joe E. Brown, a dull-witted sailor, redeems himself after he accidentally catches a spy. Most of the comedies end on an up-beat note as the misfits usually overcome their problems. These movies were apolitical with satire that could only be considered mildly anti-military.[1]

Musicals about the Navy, most of which were really musical comedies, appeared in the late 1920s with the advent of sound. Plots were similar to other comedy films, but became secondary to the music. The typical story was about a sailor on leave looking for romance. Like the straight comedy, the main character was rarely a hero. After the success of these movies, many which were "B" or second billing pictures, the major studios entered the market using top stars and lavish settings. After America's entrance into the Second World War, these films became standard fare for boosting morale at home and with the troops.[2]

SAILOR'S LADY

Twentieth Century Fox's *Sailor's Lady* released on February 12, 1940 was a preparedness comedy aimed at female audiences as well as potential recruits. A studio promotional "teaser" for the film suggests that ladies join with the Navy in their fun with "romance ashore and fun afloat." Frank W. Wead and Frederick Hazlitt Brennan, two of America's best known tellers of Navy yarns, brought the story to the screen. Wead, who wrote the screenplays for *Helldivers* (1932) and *Dive Bomber* (1941), penned the original story. Brennan, who was the author of many magazine short stories about sailors and their girls, wrote the screenplay.

This comedy, first known as *The Sweetheart of Turret One*, a very appropriate name during the the battleship era, is about the adventures of sailors and their girls. Much of the filming was done at the fleet anchorage at San Pedro, California, less than 25 miles away from Hollywood.[3] The flagship of the United States Fleet, the USS *Pennsylvania*, was used for exterior shots and the studio built sections of a battleship for filming on studio sound stages. Actors were advised and instructed on Navy routines on the flagship's quarterdeck.

More a comedy than anything else, *Sailor's Lady* also has some romantic and dramatic twists as well. The movie begins with the return of the battle fleet after a long cruise. Danny Malone (Jon Hall), a seasoned gob, is ready to marry his girlfriend Sally (Nancy Kelly), but finds out that she plans to adopt a ten-month-old baby boy named "Skipper." The cute little toddler had lost his parents in a car crash and is loved by all. Competition for the hand

---

1. Larry Langman and Ed Borg. *Encyclopedia of American War Films* (New York: Garland Publishing, Inc.) 1989. pp. 634-36.

2. *Ibid.,* pp. 386-88.

3. Battleships were frequently used as movie backgrounds at this time. *Shipmates* was filmed aboard the USS *Colorado* and *Here Comes the Navy* was filmed on the ill-fated USS *Arizona*.

The original pre-war story about the antics of sailors and their girls was written by the dean of films about the Navy, Frank W. Wead. Here gunner's mates Jon Hall and Dana Andrews discuss the fate of an orphaned toddler named "Skipper" with interested parties.

of Sally from another gob Rodney (Buster Crabbe) and the fear that the baby will be taken away keeps Sally on the move.

The prime sequence for laughs in the movie is when Sally visits the battleship *Dakota* and leaves "Skipper" in Danny's bunk in order to hide the child from authorities. Matters get frantic when the fleet unexpectedly steams out with child on board for battle practice. Luckily, the ship is commanded by a captain with a heart of gold. He parades the child before enlisted men at attention and has him escorted to port by Danny and his buddies. Happily, Danny and Sally run away with the youngster and all ends well for everyone.

Sailor's Lady is good for the Navy's image because the fun and excitement it exudes is good for enlistments. Moreover, the kindly portrayal of the ship's captain humanizes the officer's corps. One reviewer called it a "B" picture, but said that it could certainly hold its own as a supporting feature.[4]

IN THE NAVY

One service comedy that could certainly hold its own anywhere was Universal Studio's *In the Navy* released on May 28, 1941. Starring the most popular comedy team of service movies, Abbott and Costello, this film almost doubled the gross office receipts of its very popular earlier Army counterpart, *Buck Privates*. The success of *Buck Privates* had been so phenomenal (in large cities it ran only second to *Gone with the Wind*) that producer Alex

Gottlieb decided to shelve Abbott and Costello's *Hold That Ghost* in order to get ready for the potentially more lucrative *In the Navy*. Though the film was only given a so-called "B" picture budget, Arthur Horman who conceived the story and John Grant who embellished its comedy routines, tried to raise the quality of the film as best they could. Producer Gottlieb was able to save a substantial amount of money when he received permission to use naval facilities at San Pedro and San Diego as locations for the film.[5] Dick Powell, who was in a career slump, agreed to play the romantic lead only if he got top billing with the two comedians.

In the Navy was released just four months after *Buck Privates* had hit the screen. While *Buck Privates* easily had the better songs like "I'll be with You in Apple Blossom Time" and the "Boogie, Woogie, Bugle Boy," both comedies caught the popular mood of the time. Like Bob Hope's *Caught in the Draft*, it lightened the hearts of those worried about the draft and possible war. The morale of young men of draft age may well have been uplifted by the bumbling antics of characters they could both root for and feel superior to at the same time.[6] The movies may have temporarily dispelled the notion that training for war was a grim business.

The story is basically the same as the one in *Buck Private*, only the uniform and backgrounds are different. Costello stars as a nit-wit sailor Pomeroy Watson who

4. *Variety*, July 3, 1940.

5. Bob Thomas, *Bud and Lou: The Abbott and Costello Story* (Philadelphia: J. B. Lippincott Company, 1977, p. 86.

6. Larry Langman and Ed Borg. *op. cit.*, p. 511.

THE NAVY'S ALL AT SEA...WITH THOSE RIOTOUS "BUCK PRIVATES"!

They'll torpedo your troubles and blitz your blues...with waves of laughter and a barrage of boogie-woogie!

BUD ABBOTT and LOU COSTELLO
DICK POWELL
IN THE NAVY
with
The ANDREWS SISTERS
CLAIRE DODD   DICK FORAN
BUTCH and BUDDY
CONDOS BROTHERS

Directed by ARTHUR LUBIN   Associate Producer: ALEX GOTTLIEB
Original Story by Arthur T. Horman   Screen Play, Arthur T. Horman • John Grant
A UNIVERSAL PICTURE

Comedy act Abbott and Costello team up with Dick Powell to make the Navy an exciting place to be.

has never been to sea in his six years in the Navy. Abbott is his buddy "Smokey" Adams, an electrician's mate and con-artist. Dick Powell plays Tommy Halstead, a popular crooner, who is so pestered by his adoring lady fans that he disappears into the anonymity of the Navy. Following Tommy to San Diego is Dorothy Roberts (Claire Todd). Her ambition is to get a photo of the former singing star and write a sensational expose about his giving up show business. Patty, Maxene, and Laverne, the Andrew Sisters, turn up at the naval station singing the patriotic song "Off to See the World."

Everyone goes off to see the world, including Dorothy who stows away on a battleship carrying the boys to Hawaii. There are several antics on the way as the dreadnought steams towards battleship row in Pearl Harbor.

Like the old pros that they are, Abbott and Costello play the old shell game with gusto. The funniest scene in the movie is when Pomeroy goes before a committee signing up new members for the Sons of Neptune after the crossing the equator; a sailor named Dizzy (Shemp Howard) asks Pomeroy which service he likes best, "the air, the land, or the water?" When Pomeroy exclaims "give me the water!," five sailors with water in their mouths let him have it. Both Arthur Lubin, then directing the set and Lou Costello broke up into uncontrollable laughter when Lou tried the same gag on Abbott only to have it backfire. Lubin left in the footage of Pomeroy's spontaneous laughter, considering it the funniest part of the movie.

The climax of *In the Navy* is when Pomeroy puts on an oversized captain's uniform and takes the ship on wild maneuvers in order to impress Patty Andrews. The Navy, however, thought the sequence too ridiculous, making the Pacific Fleet seem foolish and refused to give final approval to the film. Panic set in at Universal City because this particular escapade was the high-light of the movie. All was saved, however, when Gottlieb got the idea that a few retakes could eliminate the Navy's displeasure. The routine would remain the same, but it would be part of a dream Pomeroy had after accidentally drinking some sleeping potion. The dream sequence ends just before a collision with the flagship is to occur. The Navy censors saw little harm to its image if the scene was only imaginary and the film was finally approved for release.[7]

Though the songs were not as successful as those in

7. Jim Mulholland, the *Abbott and Costello Book* (New York: Popular Library, 1975). p. 67.

-19-

Buck Privates, there were a lot of them. Dick Powell sings "Starlight, Starbright" and "We're in the Navy Now" very effectively and finally ends up marrying the girl reporter. The Andrew Sisters go Hawaiian with "Hula-Ba-Lua with a Boogie Syncopation" and the nasty Chief Petty Officer Dugan (Dick Foran) sings "A Sailor's Life for Me."

This wacky slapstick comedy makes the Navy seem like fun, but underneath, there are a few serious references about the United States drifting into war. For example, a speaker at the "boot camp" graduation talks about the "perilous times" in today's world. The words sung by Dick Powell in his rendition of the fiery patriotic song "We're in the Navy Now" tells us that the men of the United States Navy are the "watchdogs of liberty" who will not tolerate an adversary who won't behave. Over and over again the concept that the Navy is America's first line of defense gives Americans heart that they are well protected. This vision of America's strength is illustrated at the beginning of the film which shows a very powerful force of eight battleships steaming in formation as the backdrop for the movie's opening title and film credits.

NAVY BLUES

Warner Bros. did not produce one service musical in 1940, but changed its policy when the popularity of *Buck Privates* became known. Two new musicals *You're in the Army Now* and *Navy Blues* were promptly begun. Completed on June 10, 1941, *Navy Blues* was thematically very close to Abbott and Costellos' *In the Navy*. Like the Universal film, this motion picture was aimed at enlisting average young Americans into the Navy by showing them that the Navy was fun and romantic. In *Navy Blues*, a reason for joining up is made even clearer. Women are, it is said, simply attracted to the man in uniform. This is illustrated when seaman Cake (Jack Oakie) reasons that the best way to secure his bet on the gunnery competitions is to urge Margie (Anne Sheridan) to charm Homer (the fleet's best gun-spotter, Herbert Andersen) to stay in the Navy and win the contest. As far as Cake is concerned, "a uniform is catnip for babes."[8] The song "When Are We Going to Land Abroad," reinforces the idea that being in the Navy is a good place to romance the ladies.

While *Navy Blues* was being made, lawyers from Paramount Pictures accused Warner Bros. of using the same plot in its production that was used in their 1931 film *True to the Navy*, starring Clara Bow. While both scripts are about betting on gunnery competition between bat-

8. Production Papers. *Navy Blues, Synopsis*, November 6, 1940, Warner Bros. Archives, U.S.C.

The "Navy Blues Sextet" promoted the film around the country firmly identifying the Navy with pretty girls. Included are Peggy Diggens, Georgia Carroll, Lorraine Gettman, Marguerite Chapman, Katherine Aldridge and Claire James. © 1941 TURNER ENTERTAINMENT CO.

Jack Oakie and Jack Haley had no trouble
in finding girls in *Navy Blues*.
© 1941 TURNER ENTERTAINMENT

Jack Oakie and Jack Haley were better at
getting girls than they were at being sailors.

© 1941 TURNER ENTERTAINMENT

tleships, the screenplays are otherwise not identical.[9]
Nonetheless Warner Bros., fearing a possible lawsuit or
a loss of good will with its competitor, looked for another
kind of rivalry that battleship crews could have. They
discussed depth-charging, boxing, boat racing, and even
spitting contests. Realizing that good will between studios
was mutually beneficial, Jack L. Warner and Paramount
President Frank Freeman finally adjusted their differences
and the *Navy Blues* script was kept intact.

Navy Blues opened at the Strand Theater in New York
City, only four months after *In the Navy* hit the screen.
But the Warner Bros. picture was much weaker and was
severely panned by the critics. One reviewer wrote that
Navy Blues became a "spectacle of six comics in search
of an honest laugh."[10] Another said that *Navy Blues* did
not seem to have a script. Most of the criticism of the

picture was pointed at the four writers who collaborated
on the comedy.

Navy Blues is the story of a couple of dopey sailors
who having wagered a considerable amount of money
on a coming gunnery competition, find out that their
ace gunner Homer (Herbert Anderson) will be leaving
the Navy two days before the contest begins. They hit
on the idea that lovely Marge Jordan (Anne Sheridan)
might be the one who can charm Homer into re-enlisting.
They are correct and she entices the poor gunner into
signing up for another tour. Meanwhile, Margie falls in
love with Homer, and happily for all, his marksman-
ship wins the day for his ship. A group of show girls
called the Navy Blues Sextet liven up the picture and further identify the Navy with pretty girls.

9. Warner Bros. Intercommunications between McDermid and Bringer,
Feb. 12, 1941. Production papers, *Navy Blues*, Warner Bros. Archives. U.S.C.

10. *New York Times*, Sept. 20, 1941.

SAILOR'S ON LEAVE

Patriotism, fun, and girls is also the theme of two other musicals which flooded the cinema world before the Pearl Harbor attack. They are Republic's *Sailor's on Leave* and Paramount's *The Fleet's In*. *Sailor's on Leave* was released on October 2, 1941. With its battleship and cafe settings, the story is about a sailor who is heavily in debt to the crew members of his ship. The sailor, Chuck Stephens (William Lundigan) hates women, but his buddies jokingly fake a marriage between him and a cafe singer, Linda Hall (Shirley Ross). But shipmates that have it in for Stephens fix it so that the marriage is real. Linda falls for the sailor and everything is righted when he gets a reward for recovering stolen jewelry and can pay his creditors off. Four songs by Jules Styne and Frank Loesser help the picture considerably. They are "Because We Are Americans," "Since You," "Sentimental Folks," and "When a Sailor Goes Ashore."

THE FLEET'S IN

Though it was not released until January 1942, *The Fleet's In* was conceived and produced as a typical pre-war musical comedy. The Navy only acts as a background to the more important musical and romantic aspects of the script. Casey Kirby, a shy sailor (William Holden) gets a reputation as the fleet's Lothario when he accidentally is kissed by a movie star. Casey's reputation skyrockets when the admiral's daughter also kisses him when he asks the movie star to her party. This amazes Jake (Leif Erickson), known as the number one ladies' man in the fleet. Not to be out done, he boasts that he knows a lady who is impervious to the charm of sailors and will not be kissed in public. After hearing this, Casey's friend Barney (Eddie Bracken) bets Jake that Casey will be able to kiss this woman known as the "Countess" (Dorothy Lamour). When the fleet pulls into San Francisco, Casey and Barney find the Countess and try to win the bet. She likes Casey, but is disturbed when she hears rumors he will give her a cheap engagement ring just to get a kiss in public. A fracas occurs at the nightclub where she works and Casey is arrested. The Countess's testimony helps Casey in court. As the fleet prepares to depart, a parson arrives in a cab and marries Casey and the Countess. Barney wins the bet when the two lovers kiss each other in full view of the men of the fleet.

Band Leader Jimmy Dorsey's music is a notable segment of this simple movie. Two songs *Tangerine* and *I Remember You* are considered among the best standard tunes fifty years later. The title song "The Fleet's In" writ-

ten by Victor Schertzinger with words by Johnny Mercer tells the audience, particularly the girls, that sailors are fun in a carefree musical way. The bond between sailors and girls is at the heart of the lyrics in this spirited song:

Hey there Mister! You'd better hide you sister,
'cause the fleet's in, the fleet's in,
Hey there Mister! Don't say nobody's kissed her,
'cause the fleet's in, the fleet's in.
If they do as well on the sea
as they do on shore, Hey there Congress!
You can tax us some more (Get me, I'm only kiddn')
Hey there, rookie! You'd better call your cookie
and your sweets in, the fleet's in,
They'll take anything if it isn't nailed down
She may be dark or fair those sailors don't care as long
as she's wearing a gown
So if you love her keep under cover the fleet's in town![11]

11. "The Fleet's In," Famous Music Corp., 1942.

Betty Hutton, Eddie Bracken, Dorothy Lamour and William Holden enjoying themselves in San Francisco, a popular West Coast liberty town.

Excited sailors watch Dorothy Lamour aboard their ship. The *Arizona* is anchored in the background.

4

WORLD WAR II

Dramas and Musicals, 1942-1945

The Pearl Harbor attack on December 7, 1941, stunned the American film community as it did most Americans. While some studios had already cooperated with the government in alerting the American people to the danger of war, Hollywood's new wartime tasks would need to be greatly expanded. The movie industry's role now was to help the American people understand the meaning of the war and thus inspire the unity and purpose needed for victory. Because many film makers did not know how to begin this complicated undertaking, few good war films were produced during the first year of the war. Films which concentrated on less important events such as espionage and spying seemed to gain in ascendancy, while films looking into the ideological and military aspects of the war were neglected. Though there were inspirational stories that could be made into motion pictures, few were produced. A possible problem was that films that took a long time to make risked losing their topicality. Paramount's *Wake Island* was an exception. Released in September 1942, it was nominated for an Academy Award as the best picture of the year.

Playing it safe, Hollywood film companies continued on with the old familiar formulas in making service comedies and musicals. Low-budget war movies that exploited current headlines were added to their agendas. This was the way that producers felt they could do well at the box office. Many films implied topicality with "catchy" titles such as *Remember Pearl Harbor*, but were bereft of any content about the subject of the title. Another factor hindering the production of good war movies was the unavailability of assistance from the military. The first year of the war was mainly defensive and the Army and Navy had their hands full. As a result, most war films were small-scale fictionalized stories about war that were only slightly based on historical fact. Thus, films such as Columbia's *Submarine Raider* and RKO's *The Navy Comes Through* made in 1942 are scarcely remembered today.[1]

There was an inevitable reaction to these kinds of movies from the public and the government's own media watchdog, the Office of War Information. According to Bowsley Crowther, the movie critic for the *New York Times*, the people were not so much "tired of war's realities," but of (the) woefully cheap make-believe," they saw on the screen.[2] The government was so dissatisfied with the job Hollywood was doing that they required motion picture executives to view the government documentaries like Frank Capra's *Why We Fight* and learn from them. These pressures affected the movie-makers and by the end of the second year of the war, some films about the fighting forces were beginning to turn away from much of their simplistic, flag-waving and romantic heritage. Infused with a greater understanding of combat and violent death of war, 1943 saw the production of a more mature war film making its appearance.

Of the 95 pictures made about the fighting forces during the three years between 1942 and 1944, 51 or 53.75% were made about the Army, 26 or 27.35% about the Navy, 8 or 8.45% about the Merchant Marine, 5 or 5.3% about women's units, and 5 miscellaneous films or 5.3%. The proportion of Army to Navy films was two to one, but almost half of the Navy pictures (12 in a three year total of 26) depicted the marines. The primary emphasis in Army films was training, with two training pictures made for every one about combat. The Navy ratio was reversed with two combat films for every film about training.[3]

SUBMARINE RAIDER

Columbia's *Submarine Raider* completed on March

---

1. Jeanine Basinger, *The World War II Combat Film: Anatomy of a Genre.* (New York: Columbia University Press, 1986), p. 36.

2. Quoted in Lewis Jacob's "World War II and the American Film." *Cinema Journal*, Volume III, Winter 1967-68, p. 13.

3. Dorothy B. Jones. "The Hollywood War Film, 1942-44," *Hollywood Quarterly*, Vol. 1, No. 1. October 1945, p. 12.

12, 1942, just three months after America's entrance into World War II, was Hollywood's first film about the Navy that featured some combat. Though the combat is fictional, the attack on Pearl Harbor which the movie is about is not. The film is only 65 minutes long and shows no evidence that any technical help was given by the Navy.

Submarine Raider is about an American submarine's unsuccessful attempt to warn Pearl Harbor of an impending Japanese air attack. As the carriers approach Hawaii, one of them can't resist sinking an unarmed pleasure craft. A victim in this dastardly deed Sue Curry (Marguerite Chapman) is the only survivor and is picked up by an American submarine. The action sequences in this film are so dominant that there is little for the actors to do. Despite Miss Chapman's charm, there is never a hint of romance. Meanwhile, the American submarine frantically tries to warn authorities on Oahu of an impending disaster, but the messages are jammed by the Japanese. A very suspicious governor of Hawaii is seized by Japanese fifth columnists. With the success of the attack now history, the Japanese carrier *Hiranomo* heads for home, but is tracked by the unforgiving American submarine. In a New York City theater showing the picture, an all-male audience applauded cheerfully as the carrier receives three American torpedoes and slips under the waves, rising sun emblem and all.

The whole production seems cheaply done and contrived. Despite good shots of the submarine interior (possibly borrowed from another studio), there is a lot wrong with the studio's special effects. The battle sequence between the sub and the Japanese aircraft carrier is handled with uncertainty. The Japanese carrier maneuvers more like a raft than a man o' war. She quite clearly sits still in the water as the three American torpedoes approach. The movie's miniatures, especially the attacking Japanese planes seem phony as well. The over-made-up Japanese carrier captain played by actor Nino Pepitone is out-right laughable.

THE NAVY COMES THROUGH

The Navy Comes Through was another attempt by Hollywood to depict naval action during 1942. This RKO production was released on November 12, 1942. A time lag between the making of a feature film and the events themselves precluded the release of the films about the great naval battle like the Coral Sea and Midway that had already taken place that year. Government sponsored documentary films like John Ford's *Battle of Midway* were more timely. Over 500 copies of the *Battle of Midway* were sent around the country at government expense.

While the title and introduction of the *Navy Comes Through* shows stock shots of powerful American naval units, the film is not so much about any one battle as it is about the men who make up the Navy. In this instance, the heroes are the sailors of a Navy gun crew assigned to protect a merchant ship. The men of the merchant marine are praised as well. The gun crew is typically American—there is an ethnic Irishman and recent immigrants from Cuba and Austria. These men carry popular American interests with them like baseball and operating ham radios. They seem fearless and good natured.

The story is about a young naval officer named Sands (George Murphy) who is accused of dereliction of duty in an earlier gunnery accident. Testifying against him was Chief Petty Officer Mallory (Pat O Brien) who was

Eddie Laughton, Bruce Bennett, John Howard, Marguerite Chapman and Forrest Tucker in a scene from *Submarine Raider*.

In 1942, finding actors to play the Japanese enemy was no easy task. Here we find Nino Pepitone, of Italian descent, and Phillip Ahn, a Korean, cast as Japanese naval officers.

The Navy Comes Through, 1942, features an all-American gun crew on board a merchant ship. Pat O'Brien, George Murphy, Jackie Cooper and Desi Arnaz are ready for action.

sure of Sand's carelessness. Sands and Mallory are further estranged because Mallory's sister Myra (Jan Wyatt) is in love with Sands. Sands is forced to resign his commission, but returns to the Navy as an enlisted man after Pearl Harbor. After finishing naval "boot camp" (he is an Annapolis graduate), he is unfortunately assigned to Mallory's gun crew, a unit aboard the sleazy old merchantman, *Sybil Gray*.

Events begin to move quickly when the freighter and its Navy gun crew are ordered to join a convoy in the North Atlantic. There is a fight between the freighter and a Nazi U-Boat and the continuing bickering between Mallory and Sands. The conflict between the two men grows more intense when Myra is sent to the ship to nurse a wounded crew member. Sands is again wrongfully accused of dereliction of duty.

The *Sybil Gray* appears to be able to cope with the Germans quite well, especially after a young ham radio operator (Jackie Cooper) unscrambles the German code and finds out where a German supply ship is supposed to rendevous with the U-Boats. With the merchant skipper's permission, the old freighter tracks down the supply ship, boards it, and takes it as a prize. Sands leads the crew in placing delayed-action bombs in the torpedoes to be picked up by the unsuspecting U-Boats. The gun crew

cheers when four Nazi subs blow up. There are no doubts about Sands' heroics. He keeps the unfaltering love of Myra and finally gains the respect of her brother. In an attempt to glorify these valiant men of the sea, RKO, according to one reviewer, has instead wrecked itself "upon treacherous shoals of banality."[4]

The message, however, is clear. The Navy is made up of men of strength and versatility and this is true of the merchant marine as well. Secondly, the delivery of war materials to the fighting fronts is both hazardous and absolutely essential for victory. Finally, America's resolve to win the war is growing. The exploits of the *Sybil Gray* might seem unbelievable, but the film's basic theme comes through when Sands quotes John Paul Jones famous aphorism "We have just begun to fight."

This sea adventure was made without going to sea, and that is not easy. Studio craftsman constructed half of a full-sized prototype of the freighter *Sybil Gray* and nailed it solidly to the floor of a large sound stage, miles away from the ocean. The only body of water nearby was a couple of tanks used for splashing purposes. They set up a rocking arc lamp which projected waves on an acre or more of white muslin around its edges, making

4. *New York Times*, November 12, 1942.

everybody seasick. The principal gun used in the movie was a full-sized breech-loader which they bolted on the deck. Made exactly to Navy specifications in appearance, the materials used to build the gun were picked up at a junk yard and consisted of a piece of oil-well pipe, some old gears taken from a baking machine, and some paint. While the cost of the material was a mere $20, the completed gun was worth over $8,000 because of the many hours of hand labor put into it. Compressed air managed the gun's recoil mechanism and electricity set off the explosion.

With more war films on the line, other studios showed interest in the authentic looking prop.[5]

STAND BY FOR ACTION

Metro-Goldwyn-Mayer's *Stand By for Action* which opened on March 12, 1943, is like the *Navy Comes Through* in that both pictures concentrate on the men who make up the United States Navy. But the conflicts between the characters in *Stand By for Action* are milder and perhaps a little more believable.

Lt. Greg Masterman (Robert Taylor) and Lt. Comdr. Martin Roberts (Brian Donlevy) are at the center of this story about service aboard an over-aged, but newly commissioned destroyer, the USS *Warren*. Masterman is the ship's executive officer and Roberts is the captain. Born to a wealthy Boston family, Masterman is sure of himself and a bit cocky even though he only has a sporting knowledge of the sea. His humanistic demeanor and his need to learn the Navy's code of ethics are behind his conflict with the commanding officer. Roberts, on the other hand, is a tough sailor who has worked hard to advance in the Navy. He is a stern no-nonsense fellow who follows Navy regulations to the letter. But he is not without kindness and decency.

Both men clash over the issue of assigning Chief Johnson (Walter Brennan) to the ship. Ordered to find good men for the ship, Masterman chooses Johnson because he had been the ship's caretaker for 26 years and was a member of its original crew in the last war. Johnson knows the inner workings of the ship more than anyone and has a mystical love for her. The captain cares little for this kind of sentimentality and thinks only of the man's age. He grudgingly accepts the veteran when he reports for duty. In another instance, Masterman goes against orders and slows down the destroyer's speed as she rushes to meet a convoy. He does this in order to save Johnson, near death due to an accident. Yet when reprimanded by the convoy commander for being late, Roberts takes responsibility. His firm belief is that on a United States warship, only the captain can be held accountable for errors of judgment. In this case, Masterman considers the "one over the many principle," while Roberts would argue that the slower speed could have brought destruction to every man on the ship or even the convoy.

The film makes a definite break from its combat mode when the destroyer picks up a life-boat containing two men, twenty babies, and two pregnant women. This sharp contrast with the combat scenes will probably be appreciated by some in the audience who don't like war movies. The sailors are now removed from their traditional concerns and under Masterman's supervision, they do a splendid job of feeding and diapering the tiny tots, doing so in ship-shape fashion. Admiral Thomas (Charles Laughton) is thunder-struck when he observes what appears to be a pig-pen on the *Warren's* deck as she approaches the convoy. He is even more amazed when he sees that he has really been viewing a make-shift babies' play-pen instead. With this momentary pause from the realities of war, the crew turns its attention towards the birth of two babies aboard the destroyer. Even the admiral is anxious to know whether they will be boys or girls.

The picture's special effects department under A. Arnold Gillespie do their best to create an authentic naval battle in the film's last sequence. Yet while the ship models are realistic as they move in the water, the Japanese sailors on the bridge of a battleship wearing German helmets are distracting. When the admiral's flagship is disabled, the defense of the convoy is left to the *Warren*. Roberts orders a torpedo attack on the Japanese battleship which seems suicidal to Masterman. Masterman is told by the captain that command decisions are not to be influenced by personal feelings. When the executive officer reminds him that the lives of the children are at stake, he heeds the now wounded captain's orders and continues the attack. Using a smoke screen, the *Warren* doubles back and sinks the battleship. The picture's climatic line is heard just after the close of the battle when the admiral is handed a message from the victorious destroyer. Before reading it to his staff, he announces that the dispatch may well be as famous as Perry's immortal words: "We have met the enemy and they are ours." The admiral is both surprised and delighted when he reads instead "It's a boy!" Apparently, one of the women on the *Warren* had given birth.

The film got mixed reviews from the press with one critic writing that the military action in the movie was worth the price of admission. Another writer, however, fretted that the film's mock heroics would only bring complacency about the war and was an insult to the American fighting man.[6]

5. *Hollywood Citizen News*, June 27, 1942.

6. *New York Times*, March 12, 1943, p. 25.

Stand By For Action helped reestablish the concept of the convoy first used in World War I.

CRASH DIVE

Twentieth Century Fox's *Crash Dive* which was released in early 1943 was also criticized as a typical Hollywood war film of the time. While its action footage was good enough to get an Academy Award nomination for special effects, it too treats war in a romantic unrealistic fashion.

Simply stated, this story revolves around a love triangle between submarine skipper Cmdr. Connors (Dana Andrews), his fiancee Jean (Anne Baxter) and the sub's executive officer Lt. Ward Stewart (Tyrone Power). What seems incredible is that neither of the men seem to know about this strange relationship until very late in the movie. For example, the script conveniently removes Connors from the sub base at New London and sends him to Washington D.C. Jean does not tell Stewart that she is engaged to Connor and he romances her until they fall madly in love. It is only after Stewart spots Jean's picture in Connors' room and Connors overhears Stewart and Jean professing their love for each other that both men realize what is happening. This occurs when the submarine is being readied for its second cruise.

The special effects of the battle scenes are spectacular, but the war itself does not seem real. The ease with which the Americans win each encounter is due to the propagandistic nature of the film. In the first action sequence, the submarine while patrolling the North Atlantic is surprised by a German Q-Boat. Connors quickly orders a crash dive to the ocean's bottom where the Americans convince the Germans that they have been sunk by send-ing up pieces of clothing and allowing some oil to reach the surface. Fooled by this clever ploy, the Germans stop their depth-charging. At this point, the Americans fire a couple of torpedoes and sink the German raider.

The mission of the sub's next cruise is to find a Nazi U-Boat base in the Atlantic somewhere on "a northern coast." Like the earlier film *Submarine Patrol*, submarine bases like these lack realism and an attack on them is absurd. It is known that U-Boat bases in the Second World War were in occupied Europe and were highly fortified. The tension on this patrol is further exacerbated by the continuing friction the men are having over Jean. They finally find the U-Boat base by following a German tanker through mine fields and nets. Stewart is ordered to take a commando team ashore and destroy the enemy's installations. When the attack on the base commences, Connors will begin sinking enemy shipping. One line brings down the house when the commandos prepare to leave the sub. The black cook (Ron Carter) walking among the men as they darken their faces for the assault says "seems I'm the only natural commando aboard." The raid is a great success and they maneuver their way through the nets to safety.

Back in New London, Connors breaks off his engagement with Jean. This is never satisfactorily explained and once again we see how love and human-interest sub-plots don't have a life of their own, but are merely tacked on the main theme of naval combat. The screenwriters may have felt some light relief was needed.

The Navy cooperated with the film company and opened its New London training facilities where many

Tyrone Power leads a group of submariners in a daring attempt to destroy a U-boat base.

Appended to the action movie *Crash Dive* is a secondary plot that artificially pits Tyrone Power against Dana Andrews for the hand of Anne Baxter.

sequences were shot. Recording movie dialogues in the interior of a submarine was a problem because the insides of subs are like a barrel with sound echoing and bouncing around. When, for example, Connors says "fire one," the echo comes back "one, one, one," four or five times. Studio sound man Barney Fredericks partially solved the problem by placing elaborate softening filters on his own equipment and placing rolled socks, clothing, and other pieces of cloth behind the machinery if it could be concealed.[7]

The combat scene in *Crash Dive* are among the most authentic yet seen on the screen. This was achieved by filming real submarine exteriors and interiors and using authentic looking mock-ups of enemy surface ships and installations.

DESTROYER

In the Columbia motion picture *Destroyer* which was reviewed in New York City on September 23, 1943, Edward G. Robinson portrays an older World War I Navy vet who wants to serve on the newly built destroyer *John Paul Jones*, the namesake of his old ship. This is essentially the same idea seen in the Walter Brennan character in *Stand By for Action*, another tale about destroyers. Both men represent Americans who had fought a vicious enemy in World War I and were willing to do it again. The early war song "We Did it Before and We Can Do it Again" with its lyrical reference "putting the ax to the Axis," is a musical expression of the theme and a subplot in the two destroyer movies.[8]

Destroyer is another film about the Navy written by screenwriter Frank W. Wead. This yarn is about the workhorse of the fleet, the destroyer. These ships are occasionally referred to as "Tin Cans." As the "busy-bodies" of the fleet, they bore the brunt of numerous naval engagements and were named, not unreasonably after American war heroes. In this case, the fictitious ship was the USS *John Paul Jones*. The screenplay follows a natural sequence of events which show the building, and the launching of the destroyer, the selection and training of its crew, life ashore and aboard the craft, her shakedown cruise, and finally her valiant action against the enemy.

Edward G. Robinson (Steven Boleslavaski or "Boley") has a spirited devotion to the *Jones* that is intense. As a welder, he gives his utmost to make the ship perfect. After she is launched (his daughter Mary does the launching), "Boley" meets Lt. Cmdr. Clark, his shipmate from the first *Jones* who is now the captain of the second one. He is fired up enough to rejoin the Navy and serve on the new destroyer he helped build. From the beginning, "Boley" finds a generational difference between his spirited "old Navy" values and the younger men who don't understand his enthusiasm. He is made Chief Boatswain's mate over a younger man, Mickey Donohue (Glenn Ford) who had first been chosen for this assignment. "Boley" wins the never-ending contempt of Donohue and matters are made worse when the younger man falls in love with "Boley's" daughter Mary (Marguerite Chapman). Despite a breakdown in the ship's propulsion system and an order relegating the destroyer to mail duty, "Boley" still loves

7. Production Files, *Crash Dive*, Academy of Motion Picture Arts & Sciences, Margaret Herrick Library, Beverly Hills, CA.

8. Cliff Friend and Charles Tobias, "We Did it Before and We Can Do it Again," M. Witmark 7 Sons, 1941.

Marguerite Chapman, Glenn Ford and Edward G. Robinson as they appear in Columbia's production *Destroyer.*

A proud chief petty officer (Edward G. Robinson) meets new recruits as they arrive at "boot camp." Edgar Buchanan (left) brings mechanical skills to the Navy, while Leo Gorcey (right) looks like he might have an attitude problem.

Chief Edward G. Robinson offers a higher rating to his buddy Edgar Buchanan.

the *Jones*. Many crew men are irritated by "Boley's" continued harping on naval traditions and ask to transfer. He even loses his rating to Donohue. It is not until the mail-carrying destroyer unexpectedly meets a Japanese force in the waters of the northern Pacific that "Boley's" real worth becomes known. This is seen when the *Jones* takes a torpedo and lists dangerously. "Boley" and Donohue try to save the ship, but it is "Boley's" herculean underseas welding job that saves the day. The crew is impressed with his daring and skill and the captain later presents him with the ship's commissioning pennant.

One may ask if movies being made at the same time as an on-going battle ever incorporates scenes, ideas, or sequences from that naval action. A case in point is the the Battle of Komandorski Islands which was fought in the early Spring of 1943 while the film *Destroyer* was being made. Two American cruisers, and four destroyers took part in this gun fight. A significant occurrence in the war because the battle ended the Japanese threat to Aleutians,[9] a fictionalized version of this event which included the *Jones* might have helped Americans learn about the parameters of Pacific War. Perhaps the morale of the American people could have been lifted. The exigencies of the war, however, and the pace of studio production precluded this from ever happening. The Navy did not report the battle results for well over a month; studios could not quickly change the scripts or produce mock-ups or other props. So the time factor prevented *Destroyer* from laying out an understanding of the Pacific War for the public. A film that did a much better job in authenticating naval operations on the screen during the war was *Destination Tokyo* which was released in early 1944.

DESTINATION TOKYO

1943 was to be a pivotal year in the production of war films about the Navy. The Navy now had the where-with-all to lend the studios a helping hand with equipment and naval victories in the Pacific were an excellent source for new material. The film *Destination Tokyo* was an example of the return of close cooperation between the studios and the Navy. Film critics hailed the motion picture enthusiastically. Warner Bros. and the Navy were now ready to pool their resources to make a movie about submarine operations in the Pacific. First entitled "West to Japan," in an article in *Life Magazine*, *Destination Tokyo* was the first big budget movie of the war which clearly established the world of the combat submarine. According to film writer Jeanine Basinger, "The challenge of limited space to be explored by the camera, coupled with various possibilities for dramatic action—both above and below the sea—make it (*Destination Tokyo*) a natural for the film medium."[10]

Screenwriter Delmer Daves was the single most important person in the making of the film. Daves chose to both write and direct the picture because he felt that this was the only way he could preserve the tone of his screenplay.[11] Trained as a lawyer at Stanford University, Daves was a "Renaissance Man," who possessed knowledge and interests in many fields. He was keenly interested in scientific illustrations and taught that subject at Stanford. His devotion to detail and his yearning for authenticity on the screen may be the result of this experience. The accuracy of his reproduction of still-secret radar equipment so startled Navy Intelligence that they demanded to know Daves' source of information. Daves simply told them that his "Radar" was based on a different technology than the Navy's and for that reason the Navy's security would not be compromised.[12]

Edward G. Robinson poses by the main armament of his destroyer.

9. John A. Lorelli, *The Battle of the Komandorski Islands* (Annapolis Naval Institute Press, 1984). *supra.*

10. Jeanine Basinger, *The World War II Combat Film: Anatomy of a Genre*, New York: Columbia University Press), 1986, p. 63.

11. *Variety*, August 8, 1977.

12. Lawrence H. Suid, *Guts and Glory: Great American War Movies* (Reading: Addison-Wesley Publishing Company, 1978), p. 55.

Japanese intelligence authorities have become aware of the presence of an American submarine in *Destination Tokyo.*

Delmer Daves had come to Hollywood in the early 1930s to become an actor, but soon switched to screen writing. He wrote the screenplay for *Shipmates* in 1932 and *Shipmates Forever* in 1934. His fondness for detail and accuracy were apparent in his staging of Change of Command Ceremonies in both *Shipmates Forever* and later in *Task Force* with Gary Cooper playing an admiral giving up his command.

Daves did a lot of preparation for the movie *Destination Tokyo.* He spent one week at the submarine base at Mare Island, California gathering information, interviewing sailors, and developing incidents for the movie. Members of the cast were asked to attend regular Navy classes and spent two days learning how to go in and out of submarine hatches. He got permission from the Navy to use a layout of a modern submarine and brought back scaled drawings for studio use.[13] Studio technicians built forward and aft torpedo rooms, officer cubicles, engine and battery rooms, and the crew's quarters, all to Navy specifications without revealing any secrets. The USS *Copperfin,* the name of the movie's fictionalized

underseas raider, became a submarine in every sense of the word, except it lacked the capability to go to sea.[14]

Destination Tokyo opened at the *Strand* Theater in New York City on January 1, 1944. The story is about an American submarine which secretly brings to the shores of Japan a meteorologist whose mission is to send weather information to General Doolittle in preparation for his daring raid on Tokyo in April 1942. Many things happen as the submarine makes its way to Japan. The *Copperfin* is attacked by a Japanese plane leaving the Aleutian Islands and the thinnest man on the sub must defuse an unexploded bomb as the crew waits in suspense. The sub slips through nets and minefields into Tokyo Bay, lands the meteorologist, and successfully retrieves him. At the same time, a member of the crew undergoes an appendectomy done by an inexperienced pharmacist mate. They witness the Doolittle Raid, sink a Japanese carrier, and undergo a horrific depth-charging as they

13. *New York Herald Tribune,* January 2, 1944.

14. Production Notes, *Destination Tokyo,* December 7, 1943. Warner Bros. Archives, U.S.C.

John Garfield and other typically American crew members of the *Copperfin* admire the opposite sex in any form.

Plans are made to land a meteorologist who will gather information needed for the forthcoming Doolittle Tokyo Raid.

Cary Grant plays the idealized submarine captain who is aware of the consequences of enemy detection.

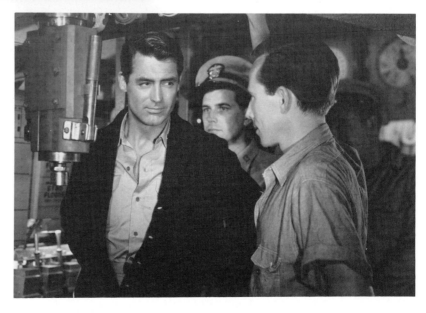

make their way to the safety of the open sea. While no single American submarine did all of these things alone, events in the picture actually happened or could have happened.

The depiction of the crew of the *Copperfin* both captures and projects the spirit of wartime America. Captain Cassidy (Gary Grant) is a resourceful and cunning commander who becomes a father-figure to his men. A true submariner, he wears an officer's hat with a plain visor instead of a gold-braided one. He does not want to remind himself or others that the higher rank means a desk job in the future. He is fundamentally a good man whose only conflict is with the Japanese. The crew is portrayed as a family made up of diverse individuals who learn how to work together despite the danger of disaster and death associated with the submarine service. Mike (Tom Tully) is an Irish-American who listens to his wife's voice on the phonograph as he retires to the ship's recreation office; young Tommy Adams (Robert Hutton) maintains contact with his family by displaying a picture of his sister,

while other sailors do the same thing with their wives and girlfriends. "Tin-can" (Dana Clark), a Greek-American sees himself as the avenger of his honored uncle's execution at the hands of the Nazis. The entire crew shares the sense of loss when one of their compatriots is stabbed to death by a Japanese pilot he was trying to rescue. The men are regular guys who celebrate Christmas by singing carols and exchanging gifts. They pray a lot and play *Home on the Range* on the loud-speaker system. They are true American warriors, basically good-natured, but resourceful and willing to put their lives on the line for their country.

Producer Jerry Wald was pleased with Daves' first draft script, but felt that it lacked enough ideological fervor. The fundamental nature of the script's direction was not changed, but he had writer Albert Maltz write in some dialogue about the nature of the war in the script. For example, Maltz has captain Cassidy scorn America's prewar isolationists when he tells the crew that "appeasement has come to roost" when he shows them a Japanese

The meteorologist and others leave the studio-constructed submarine in dangerous waters.

bomb detonator cap which has "Made in the USA" stamped on it. This shows us that the isolationists had earlier sided with America's enemies. Cassidy also tells his men that Japanese society is an unbalanced one because of its militarism and lack of labor unions. But he hastens to add that it is not the Japanese people who are at fault; it is their system of government. In an anti-fascist sequence, "Tin-can" tells his shipmates that he hates Nazism because it denies intellectual freedom and the right of human beings to live and die peacefully. Both of these scenes would not have been in the motion picture had Maltz not been hired to put a little ideological bite into the script. Daves' mastery in describing life on a submarine and Maltz's explanation of why the United States was at war may explain why *Destination Tokyo* was both a success at the box office and a fondly remembered film.

THE FIGHTING SEABEES
. . . .

The *Fighting Seabees* starring John Wayne unfortunately reverts back to the earlier type of war films in which sub-plots are added in order to enhance the film's commercial success. While the idea of making a film about the creation of the Navy's Construction Battalions (Seabees) is a good one, studio insistence in bringing in a romantic interlude was not. Wayne thought the movie had great possibilities when he first read the script, but later bemoaned the fact that the addition of the love story took the reality out of it.[15] This high-budgeted film was finished on December 5, 1943, and previewed on January 17, 1944. This was only two weeks after *Destination Tokyo* opened. While *New York Times* critic Bowsley Crowther praised the submarine film as a "pippin of a picture from a purely dramatic point of view," another writer wrote that the *Fighting Seabees* was just another Hollywood movie made along the lines of a standardized western. In an ad in *Variety*, Wayne's movie was announced as the "Money-making picture of the year."[16] It did gross almost $400,000 in just under two months.

Though marred by a love triangle between a hot-heated construction boss Wedge Donovan (John Wayne) and his naval superior Bob Yarrow (Dennis O'Keefe) over the affections of reporter Constance Chesley (Susan Hayward), the picture does have time to salute the courageous efforts of the Seabees. The story begins when Wedge meets his men returning from a construction job on a Pacific island. He is dismayed when he sees their wounds and finds out that they have been put at an unfair advantage because under international law, they can not be armed in a war zone. Bob Yarrow is interested in the problem and he wants these construction workers to receive Navy basic training. Both Wedge and Yarrow go to Washington,

but Wedge balks at the idea of an intensive training program for his men. Both men are sent to an embattled island and find reporter Chelsey of the same opinion as Yarrow. As she makes her plea, she finds herself falling in love with Wedge.

Some of the battles on the island are spectacular, but gruesome. First Wedge takes a group of his untrained workers on an unauthorized raid against the Japanese. He is greatly maddened when he loses many men and learns that the action has compromised Yarrow's plan to trap the enemy. Wedge returns to Washington to help form the Seabees. After training on the West Coast, Wedge and fighting Seabees are sent to another island fully armed and ready to build docks, airfields, oil depots, and warehouses. When one of his best men is killed by a sniper, Wedge defies orders again and decides to take on the enemy with his own men. The most striking scene in the picture is when Wedge, in a burst of heroism, crashes his bulldozer into an oil storage tank and burns the enemy to death in a torrent of flaming oil. The Japanese are stopped, but Wedge is killed in action. The frenzied fighting spirit in the encounter comes from an intense hatred of the Japanese, referred to in the film as "bug-eyed monkeys."

Obviously the action makes things easier for Chesley who no longer has to make a choice between the two men in her life. The last scene in the film shows the lady reporter and Yarrow standing together as they view a ceremony honoring the valor of Wedge and other Seabees killed in the Pacific War.

WING AND A PRAYER
. . . .

Twentieth Century Fox's *Wing and a Prayer* presents the aircraft carrier as the primary naval weapon in the Pacific War. Absent in this film are the phony heroics and sub-plots which have often distorted other war movies. This is the story of one of the America aircraft carriers spared during the Pearl Harbor attack because it was not in port. These ships became the back-bone of the reduced fleet which finally stopped the Japanese advance in the Pacific. This carrier is designated in the movie as Carrier X for security reasons. The real American battle-readiness was not known by the Japanese three months after Pearl Harbor. It was therefore the American intention to confuse them by restraining ship movements and convincing them that the fleet was scattered and weak. If they believed this, it was thought that a Japanese force

15. Suid, *op. cit*, p. 219.

16. *Variety*, February 28, 1944.

Marines landing on a Pacific island, to be followed by Seabees.

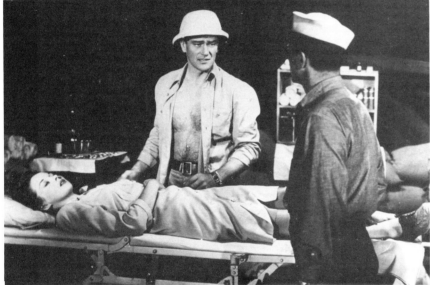

In the 1944 movie *Fighting Seabees* John Wayne is agitated over the illness of Susan Hayward on a remote Pacific island.

would again venture into the Eastern Pacific (Midway, Hawaii) and be taken by surprise by a smaller, but battle-ready American force. The film was previewed on July 12, 1944.

There is discontent on Carrier X, however. The air crews are ordered to not fight back so as to persuade the enemy of the American weakness. It is not clear if the crews are told why they are disengaging. For this and other reasons, Comdr. Harper (Don Ameche) the air officer is unpopular with the men. He scolds Oscar Scott (William Eythe) when the young pilot makes a landing after having been waved off. He grounds Ensign Brainerd (Henry Morgan) because he goes against orders and destroys a target. Yet this rigid and stern man knows what

he is doing and the squadron is trained to fight well. Lt. Comdr. Moulton (Dana Andrews) is an easier-going officer who has gained the respect of the pilots. It is Harper and not Moulton who must order radio silence at a time when one of his pilots is lost and needs his bearings.

The men are joyous when Captain Waddel (Charles Bickford) gets orders that allows Carrier X to engage the enemy, and the Battle of Midway begins. The script was to have depicted the heroic, but futile attempt by Torpedo Squadron 8 to sink a Japanese carrier. Only one man survived out of 32. Though the original story was based on the lone survivor Ensign George Gay, Navy censors changed the script, believing that this aspect of the battle was too defeatist. In retrospect, the sequence could

Pilot William Eythe is reprimanded by Carrier X's air officer Don Ameche for failing to adhere to landing instructions in Fox's *Wing and a Prayer*.

William Eythe and two crew members prepare for a mission in their TBF *Avenger*. The scene was shot on an outdoor concrete flight deck made for the movie at Twentieth Century Fox's studio in West Los Angeles.

have been included because the action of Torpedo 8 helped bring victory, not defeat. The Japanese forces concentrated on American low flying aircraft and allowed an opening for the higher flying dive bombers to obliterate their carriers. While the victory at Midway owes a lot to Torpedo 8, it may have been too gruesome for audiences to see all but one airman die, especially when the characters of these men were so well-developed in the story. In the movie, Torpedo Squadron 8's name was changed to Torpedo Squadron 5.

Following the standards set by *Destination Tokyo*, the picture was made as authentically as possible. Most of the work was done at Fox Studio at a great expense. The studio constructed a replica of an aircraft carrier costing $60,000, placing it adjacent to its lot. Set designer Lew Greber also supervised the building of 36 separate sets including a replica of a pilot's ready room, the captain's bridge and the crew's quarters. An approximately 400 foot long flight deck was designed for exterior scenes. On it were 40mm guns, a cat walk, an arresting gear, and a landing area. Much of the furnishings for the interior quarters of the ship were requisitioned from the Oakland Naval Supply Depot.

Some of the filming was done aboard the newly commissioned carrier USS *Yorktown* (CV-10). Director Henry Hathaway and five other men from Fox were allowed to sail with the ship for seven weeks on a shakedown cruise. They brought back excellent shots of take-offs, landings, and even some crash landings.

Fox was able to use a mixed number of F-6F-3s (Hell-cats), TBFs (Avengers) and SB2Cs (Helldivers), all first line Navy planes for the production. The planes were first flown from San Diego to Clover Field in Santa Monica and taxied down Pico Boulevard with a motorcycle escort to Fox's back lot. They remained on a concrete flight deck for the duration of the filming.[17]

Some of the combat scenes were not the result of studio effort alone but were drawn from real footage shot during an intense and determined Japanese attack. One such sequence showed a Japanese bomber dropping a 1,000 pound bomb near a carrier sending geysers of water at least a hundred feet. Actual battle sounds were also used in the film. Real conversation between the pilots came over the loud speakers describing the stirring combat between the Navy planes and the enemy Zeros in a running fight. Yet the difference between the sequences shot in combat and at the studio are hardly noticeable. It was not unusual for officers visiting the sets to express surprise at the authenticity of the carrier replica that served as the setting of the story.

Formal production of the picture began on February 7, 1944, and it was finished in three months. The film premiered in August 1944 and writer Jerome Cady received an Academy Award nomination for best original story.

THE FIGHTING SULLIVANS

The motion picture the *Fighting Sullivans* released in 1944 is not thought of as a war film in the general sense. It is more about the growing-up and family life of five Waterloo, Iowa, brothers who were killed in action when the Cruiser USS *Juneau* blew up near Guadalcanal in November 1942. The war service of the five men and their fiery death takes up only a small portion of the last reel of the film. The film is more of a tribute to American families and their personal sacrifices more than anything else.

The five Sullivan boys grew up in a family of modest means in a small town in Iowa. Their father was a railroad man and their mother was a homemaker. The first part of the picture tells us about their boyhood, mainly their pranks, adventures, and most important of all their strong bond as a family. Ironically enough, their mother once warned them to never set foot in a boat again after one they had built began leaking and sank. Though most of them did not finish high school, not uncommon during the depression, they were good boys who did their family chores, worked small jobs, and were loving sons

The love and marriage of one of the Sullivan brothers played by Edward Ryan and his wife played by Anne Baxter offers romantic interest in *The Fighting Sullivans*.

and brothers.

The reaction of the family to the Pearl Harbor attack was typical of many American families. They were shocked and angry. Though the movie omits the fact that the two eldest Sullivans had enlisted in the Navy in 1937, the younger three joined them after war broke out and were all assigned to the same ship. The young men wanted to reknit their earlier tight bond and to avenge the death of one of their friends lost on the *Arizona*. At first, the Navy turned down their request to serve together, but relented when the three recruits told them that being together was a condition of their enlistment. They all became shipmates on the *Juneau*.

The tearful aspect of the film was done tactfully when a naval officer (Ward Bond) was dispatched to tell the family about the deaths of their sons. Commendably free of undue sentiment, he tells them that it is not one of their sons who was killed, "it is all five." The last scene in the picture shows the mother of the five dead sailors (Selena Royle) commissioning a new destroyer, the USS *The Sullivans* (DD-537). She does her task graciously with her husband (Thomas Mitchell) and her daughter (Trudy Marshall) in naval uniform at her side.

17. Bruce Orriss, *When Hollywood Rules the Skies* (Hawthorne. Areo Associates Inc., 1984), p. 90.

Thomas Mitchell plays the father of the five Sullivan brothers.

A scene showing the last moments on the cruiser *Juneau* before it exploded and sank, taking the Sullivan brothers with it.

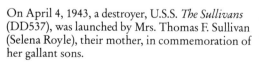

On April 4, 1943, a destroyer, U.S.S. *The Sullivans* (DD537), was launched by Mrs. Thomas F. Sullivan (Selena Royle), their mother, in commemoration of her gallant sons.

Hailed by *Film Daily* as a movie of "terrific appeal," the film did poorly at the box office until its name was changed from *The Sullivans* to *The Fighting Sullivans*. The motion picture became an unqualified success.[18]

THE STORY OF DR. WASSELL

Another successful film in 1944 was Paramount's *The Story of Dr. Wassell*. Luckily for its producer and director, Cecil B. De Mille, the movie was premiered on June 7, 1944, the day after the D-Day landing. Excitement was running high regarding this story about an unassuming Arkansas country doctor, Corydon Wassell (Gary Cooper) who as a naval officer, saved the lives of nine sailors from the cruisers *USS Marblehead and USS Houston* after the Battle of the Java Sea. So badly wounded that they could not leave on an over-crowded oiler headed for Australia, Dr. Wassell's decison to care for them undoubtedly saved their lives. It was a "fireside chat" by President Roosevelt on April 28, 1942, that made Dr. Wassell a celebrity. The president told the American people that the doctor was "almost like a Christ-like shepherd, devoted to his flock." These were desperate times for the American war effort and the president was using this act of heroism to encourage Americans to do their part to win the war. Cecil B. De Mille and Paramount saw the story's potential and decided to make a movie about it. The script took eight months to write and 143 story conferences indicating the difficulty in making the movie. Though the real Dr. Wassell was 60 years old and not very attractive, the studio signed up the popular Gary Cooper to play the part.

Dr. Wassell was a back-woods country doctor who left Arkansas for missionary work in China. He was interested in parasitology and unfortunately for him the discovery of an important disease breeding parasite carried by snails was discovered by another researcher. In flash-backs, the audience learns that he falls in love with nurse Madeline (Laraine Day), but loses her to the same man, Dr. Wayne (Lester Mathews)who had discovered the pararsite before Wassell had. Wassell leaves China and enters the Navy with a commission in the US Naval Medical Corps. He is sent to Java early in the war. The crushing defeat in the Battle of the Java Sea fills up the the Dutch medical facilities at a Javanese port. All walking-wounded are ordered to leave on the *USS Pecos*. But nine of the most severly wounded sailors are left in Java. Dr. Wassell volunteers to stay with them and courageously cares for them as the Japanese move in to capture the hospital. British troops agree to take Wassell and his sailors to catch the last ship out of Java bound for Australia. Through hor-

rendous bombing attacks which destroy needed bridges, they make it to port with practically everyone surviving. A common complaint about this film is that it has too many love stories (four in all). And the doctor's story is just a vehicle for these romances. There is Wassell's love for Madeline; a Javanese nurse's (Carol Thurston) love for a sailor; a missionary-school teacher's romance with another sailor and a Dutch nurse's (Signo Hasso) affair with a Dutch sailor. Added to this are a lot of sailors clowning around with girls in what one reviewer calls "hoopla warfare."[19] The picture was premiered at the Hollywood Paramount Theater on June 7, 1944. The entire proceeds of the Hollywood opening went to the Naval Aid Auxillary. In Dallas, Texas, a Navy Mother's convention showed the movie, prompting Navy Mother's clubs to ask to participate in a nation-wide salute to America's doctors at war. Little Rock Arkansas held a huge parade for the film showing. One Arkansas Congressman told reporters that it was "the finest picture that he had ever seen." Despite the acclaim the film got in certain quarters, some critics and military men felt that the movie distorted the reality of war. One soldier writing from a combat zone wrote that the movie was vulgar and misrepresented war for the purpose of making a spectacular epic-like display to bring people to the box-office. Film critic Bosely Crowther disliked the film so intensely that he called it a "seductive *Demili*tary display."[20]

ANCHORS AWEIGH

The *Story of Dr. Wassell* had been inspired by a "pep" talk to the American people in one of FDR's Fireside Chats in April 1942; it pictured the war in a difficult period and dramatized how courage and determination were the ingredients for victory. MGM's *Anchors Aweigh*, released in 1945, suggests another reality about the war. That is that victory is near and the Navy deserves the gratitude of the American people for a job well-done. After the picture has shown an elaborate award ceremony aboard a ship featuring Jose Iturbi conducting a massed naval band with over over a hundred musicians, each of the two heroes is awarded a Silver Star for gallantry in action. They are given a four day leave in Hollywood and are free to sing and dance their way through the rest of the film. The plot concerns the antics of the two prowling gobs in the movie capital. Aware that movies show-

18. *Film Daily*, February 3, 1944.
19. *New York Times*, June 11, 1944.
20. *New York Times*, June 7, 1944.

ing that the Navy as romantic and fun were popular, the screenwriters take the two heroes, the "Don Juanish" sailor Joe Brady (Gene Kelly) and his love-starved buddy Clarence Doolittle (Frank Sinatra) for a whirl around the exciting city. While they are there, they meet a pretty aspiring opera singer named Susan Abbott (Kathryn Grayson) who lives with her little orphaned nephew (Dean Stockwell). The sailors meet the boy while he is on his way to join the Navy all dressed up in a sailor suit. A kindly policeman (Rags Ragland) puts the fellows in charge of taking the boy home to his aunt. At first, Joe does not bother with aunt Susan- she is too straight-laced for his wolfish tastes. He turns her over to Clarence who has little experience with women and considers Joe his mentor. While the sailors are visiting Susan, a gentleman acquaintance, influential in the music business, drops in. Fearing competition, they concoct an uncomplimentary story about Susan. Her date walks out and Susan is saddened at losing this musical contact. To placate her, the sailors make up a story that they too have musical connections and that they can arrange an audition with the great Maestro Jose Iturbi. In the meantime, Clarence meets a waitress in L.A.'s Olvera Street from Brooklyn (Pamela Britton). They quickly feel comfortable with each other. This is just as well because Joe and Susan are beginning to like each other. Kelly dances well in an Olvera Street duet with a little girl and also in an animated sequence in which he tries to cheer up a little disgruntled mouse who looks like "Jerry" of "Tom and Jerry" fame. Of the songs Sinatra sings, none is very memorable except *I Fall in Love Too Easily*, which was nominated for an Oscar. Frank Sinatra surprises the audience and shows he can dance in a duo with Kelly. The sailors finally make good on their promise to get Susan an audition with Jose Iturbi. The Maestro and an audience of enlisted men of the United States Navy love her singing and her career is launched.

Once again, Hollywood's love and fun formula for films about the Navy is successsful. *Anchors Aweigh* became the third highest money-making film of that year.[21]

THIS MAN'S NAVY

Having paid tribute to the more glamorous elements of America's naval forces, Hollywood late in the war turned to making motion pictures about the less publicized branches of the Navy. One such movie was MGM's *This Man's Navy* starring Wallace Beery. Originally titled *Airship Squadron 4*, this comedy adventure portrays the Navy's LTA (lighter-than-air) squadrons, the so-called

blimps. Theater-goers had a chance to enjoy both the antics of Wallace Beery and witness the destruction of a Nazi submarine off the Atlantic Coast at the hands of a "killer" blimp. The motion picture was made in eight weeks on location at NAS Lakehurst, New Jersey, NAS Del Mar, NAS Santa Ana, and NAS Moffett Field in California where mooring practices and other operations were conducted.[22] The story is a simple one. Veteran chief petty officer and blimp pilot Trumpet (Wallace Beery) known throughout the Navy's LTA community as "old Gas Bag," loves his branch of service as well as he does telling tall tales. The unmarried Chief boasts of a non-existent son to his pal Chief Shannon (James Gleason) who has a real son. Shannon calls him a liar.

Widow Maude Weaver (Selena Royle) and her son Jess (Tom Drake) become Trumpet's surrogate wife and son when he accidentally meets them on the ranch after he bails out of his blimp. His dream of having his "son" Jess follow in his foot steps is partly dashed when he finds the young man has been crippled in a horseback riding incident. He has Navy doctors perform successful surgery in order to get Jess into the Navy. Trumpet introduces him to a lovely girl (Jan Clayton) and young Jess becomes an LTA cadet, emerging as an ensign.

Jess gets command of a blimp and a Nazi submarine is sunk. However, it is Trumpet who shows courage under fire. Jess panics. Discouraged even though his "father" covers up for him when the blimp splashes into the sea, Jess transfers to the Navy's transport command. Trumpet is then sent to the CBI (China-Burma-India) theater of war where he knows his way around. Jess, now flying transport missions around the CBI is shot down with an important British officer on board. All ends well when Trumpet rescues Jess in his LTA craft and both men reaffirm their devotion to each other. A P-38 fighter saves the day when it chases Japanese Zeros away from the harried blimp.

THEY WERE EXPENDABLE

It is ironic that one of the best motion pictures about the Navy in World War II was released only a few months after the war ended. A film of the quality of *They Were Expendable* both bolstered the spirit of the American people and further acquainted them with the realities of war. Fear that the public might lose interest in war films after the victory over Japan did not happen. The film

21. *Magills American Film Guide* (Englewood Cliffs: Salem Press, 1980) Vol. I, p. 130.

22. *Hollywood Citizen News*, May 14, 1945.

Wallace Beery at the helm of a Navy blimp hunting Nazi U-boats in MGM's *This Man's Navy*.

was not a smash hit, but it did attract large audiences.

This film which is a tribute to the valor and efficiency of the American Navy was adopted from the best selling book by the same name written three years earlier. William L. White, the author, wrote about Lt. John Buckeley and his PT-Boat squadron during the early days of the Pacific War. The three men who shaped and developed the film were all naval officers. Comdr. Frank "Spig" Wead, America's most prolific writer of Navy stories wrote the screenplay; actor Robert Montgomery who had combat experience with a PT-Boat unit, played the leading character and directed the last portion of the film and finally John Ford, the director of many feature films and documentaries, had experience with PT-Boats himself. One reviewer categorically stated that "Quite clearly the making of this picture was a labor of understanding and love."[23] It is no wonder that a British critic as late as 1950 wrote that *They Were Expendable* was "perhaps the most moving and faithful of all war films."[24]

This MGM picture is the story of the highly maneuverable yet vulnerable PT-Boats which served in the Philippines against incredible odds at the beginning of the war. Not taken seriously by the top brass, the PT-Boat squadrons are at first relegated to running errands and picket duty. As the Japanese invasion of the Philippines moves closer to success, the little boats are at last given a chance to prove their worth. Though Japanese sources

discount the boats effectiveness, the motion picture portrays them as swift and daring in battle. One scene shows a torpedo attack destroying an enemy cruiser. Both Brinkley (Robert Montgomery) and Kelly (John Wayne) fight brilliantly, but the outcome seems hopeless. Wounded in the hand, Kelly is sent to a hospital on Corregidor where he is cared for by an army nurse (Donna Reed). They fall in love, but this tender romance is ended when the squadron is ordered to carry General MacArthur to Mindanao Island for his escape to Australia. With only two boats left in the squadron, both Brinkley and Kelly continue to harass enemy shipping. They are ordered to burn their boats if attacked and both of them are finally destroyed. Both men are able to leave the Philippines and are used by the Navy to train new PT-Boat crews. The rest of the crews are trapped by superior forces, but they fight along with other American units to the bitter end.

The audience can mull over a number of vignettes in this thoughtful film. One scene is a thinly disguised depiction of MacArthur's escape from the Philippines. Ford makes the event almost reverential as the general and his entourage leave the small boats on their way to Australia. The audience knows that this is the man who will return and free the Philippines. There is no dialogue, but the

23. *New York Times*, December 26, 1945.

24. *New Statesman & Nation*, July 1, 1950.

As a competent PT-boat skipper Robert Montgomery's character understands that danger is everywhere in *They Were Expendable*.

John Wayne and Robert Montgomery use PT-boats to their best advantage.

playing of the "Battle Hymn of the Republic" in the background stirs the viewers in patriotism. Another unforgettable scene is when the old boat repair man known as "dad" plans to stand his ground with gun in hand as he waits for the advancing Japanese to come. "They won't take me without a fight," the old man insists. As in *Grapes of Wrath*, Ford shows the viewers that land is something to be fought for. At the same time, rich visions of America become manifest with the playing in the distance of a Ford favorite, "Red River Valley." The film's subtle tension between the "actual" and "staged" footage is so flawless that one cannot determine where the choreographed battle scenes begin and where the actual documentary portion takes over.

The most lasting impressions of *They Are Expendable* are not necessarily the spectacular battle scene or even the touching romance between Kelly and the sweet nurse. They are found on the faces of the people living the war. There is the baby-faced sailor allowed only to drink milk at the bar, but who is nonetheless welcomed into the military fraternity by his older buddies. One sees the look of loneliness and the weight of responsibility on the face of the squadron commander Brinkley as he ponders the fate of his men. There is despair written all over the face of an oriental lady (probably Japanese) when she hears the news about Pearl Harbor at an American officer's club. These kinds of images recall the real horror of war.

Though this film is the story of defeat, there is an underlying theme that there are more important things besides winning battles. Doing a good job, working together for the common good and never giving up are some of them.

Much of the film's camera work was done around Miami, Florida during a two month period. The rest of the work was done in Hollywood for about seven or eight weeks. The technical crew was made up of 146 people who recreated the naval bases at Manila and Cavite. The problem of how to "burn Manila" was solved when a brush fire broke out near Key Biscayne. "Perfect," said Director Ford, "That's Manila burning," and the scene was shot.[25]

It took MGM studio technicians 72 hours to duplicate what it took the Japanese less than two seconds to do in their surprise attack on the American installations around Manila. Using official Navy photos, studio special effects men turned the Miami Coast Guard station into a bomb-cratered smoldering replica of the Cavite Navy yard. Creating only an illusion of destruction, the Coast Guard station remained intact and only special break-away buildings placed around permanent structures were destroyed. Broken gas and water mains, splintered bulkheads, shattered windows, and wrecked trucks (the latter obtained

from local wrecking yards), all served to simulate the evacuation of the base.

Ex-marine Captain Jim Havens, MGM's chief explosives expert, was responsible for planting six tons of explosives in the film's action scenes. Much preparatory work was needed to film the PT-Boats running the gauntlet of Japanese gunfire. The filmed action was first charted in a blue-print showing where the charges would be located. The course of the boats was pin-pointed by a series of marker flags. The pennants were removed when the PT-Boat captains understood the sequence of events. Dynamite explosions were similarly planned on land and everyone hoped there would be no accidents. There was only one mishap and that was not caused by an explosion. Three time Academy-Award winning director John Ford slipped off a studio ladder and broke his leg. The very competent Robert Montgomery immediately took over the film's direction.[26]

25. Production papers, *They Were Expendable*, "Movie Magic Recreation Jap Manila Attack," n.d., Academy of Motion Picture Arts & Sciences, Margaret Herrick Library, Beverly Hills, CA.

26. *The Story's Dynamite, ibid.*, n.d.

THEATRE

With most of their squadron destroyed, both Montgomery and Wayne make preparations to fight to the end.

THE WAR STILL RAGES
World War II Navy Aircraft Carrier Movies, 1949-1976

The critical acclaim, yet tepid responses of audiences to *They Were Expendable* told producers that the popularity of war movies was waning. Warner Bros. suspended production of its feature film *Task Force* shortly after V.J. Day. Though war films were not discredited to the degree they were after the First World War when movie houses were obliged to tell their patrons that a particular film was not a war film, no combat picture was released in 1946. *High Barbaree* was, however, released in 1947 by MGM, but the story of the crash of a Navy PBY in the Pacific was less important in this movie than the time and place flash backs the pilot had while struggling to survive.

It was not until late 1948 that Warner Bros.' produced a combat film about the air corps entitled *Fighter Squadron*. Movies about airplanes were becoming increasingly popular and imposed fewer problems on film makers than pictures about the Army or Navy. War movies about the air war simply allowed script writers to more easily remove the main characters from combat situations and thus provide the needed flexibility to attract wider audiences.[1]

As Cold War tensions deepened in late 1949, World War II films made a substantial comeback. This was the year that the Soviet Union had exploded its first atomic bomb and China had fallen to the communists. Troubled by these events, Americans were now ready to reexamine their role in World War II. As proud victors, they wanted to know how it changed both America and the world and whether or not it was justified. Because the war had been so clear-cut and unambiguous, these films were bound to have a moral edge over later pictures about the war in Korea and Viet Nam. The United States had been, after all, at war with both the perpetrators of the attack on Pearl Harbor and the Holocaust.

A plethora of films about World War II made their appearance. In all, 31 motion pictures were made in Hollywood between 1949 and 1951. Among them were *Task Force*, *Battleground*, *Command Decision*, *Sands of Iwo Jima*, and *Twelve O' Clock High*. One of the first of these films to appear was Warner Bros.' *Task Force* which was not only about World War II, but the history of naval aviation as well. With their emphasis on the distinguished role of the aircraft carrier in the late war, both *Task Force* (1949) and later *Midway* (1976) which also accentuated carrier action, did very well at the box office.

TASK FORCE

Warner Bros. and the United States Navy pooled their considerable resources together to make *Task Force* a technically graphic and authentic account of the evolution of the Navy's air arm. Though suspended in 1945, *Task Force* was resumed in 1948 and was ready for release the next year. The time was propitious for the production of such a film. Congress was beginning its debate over military appropriations and it did not seem certain that ample money for the Navy's carrier force would be available. The Navy believed that advancing the release date of *Task Force* would help their cause because the motion picture argued that these "floating airfields" had lead to the Navy's victories in the Pacific and by implication were well suited to play a large role in the defense of the United States in the post-war world. Warner Bros. with its long history of cooperating with the Navy agreed. It also honored the Navy's request to bring the carrier story up-to-date by incorporating a modern Navy jet fly-by in the movie's last scene.[2] The simultaneous congressional hearings would certainly stimulate interest in the film. *Task Force* was first tradeshown in Los Angeles on August 23, 1949. It opened at the *Strand* theater in New York City the next week thus shortening the stay of the

---

1. Jeanine, Basinger, *The World War II Combat Film* (New York: Columbia University Press, 1986), p. 342.

2. *Variety* (d), September 29, 1949.

The extent of cooperation between Warner Bros. Studios and the Navy is seen by the appearance of a Navy band at the 1949 opening of *Task Force* at Warner's Hollywood Theater. © 1949 TURNER ENTERTAINMENT CO.

Gary Cooper flies an old VE-7 stand-in airplane illustrating early carrier operations.
© 1949 TURNER ENTERTAINMENT CO.

money-making movie *White Heat*. In turn, the Navy set up a number of airplane exhibitions in various cities around the nation to plug the picture.[3]

Task Force traces the expansion of the naval air service through the life of a fictional naval flyer Jonathan S. Scott (Gary Cooper). Scott is a kind of Hollywood Billy Mitchell type person who dedicates his life to carrier aviation. He has a tough time convincing high ranking naval officials and politicians of the importance of air power. While the intra-service rivalry in the movie between battleship admirals and carrier enthusiasts is overstated in the movie, it certainly suggests why naval air had great difficulty being funded in the inter-war period. Scott qualifies for carrier service on the USS *Langley*, but complains about the small number of planes in service. In Washington D.C., he unnerves old-fashioned admirals and isolationist senators with his outspokenness for changes in the Navy. He is given a desk job in Panama for this. But his hardships are softened, however, by his romance with Mary Morgan (Jane Wyatt) and his friendship with his Admiral McCain-like friend Pete Richard (Walter Brennan). Richard believes in the future of air power, but unlike Scott, he is less outspoken. Ordered to the carrier *Saratoga* in 1929, Scott joins a new squadron, but is hospitalized in an air crash. Mary agrees to wed Scott even though she has some fears because her first husband was killed in a crash. Their first station together is Annapolis where Scott becomes an aviation instructor. When he tries to win the midshipman over to aviation, he incurs the disfavor of the superintendent and is passed over for Commander At his wife's insistence, Scott stays in the Navy despite offers of higher pay in the civilian sector. He is with the carrier *Enterprise* at the time of Pearl Harbor and is promoted to air officer on the *Yorktown* where he will serve under his old friend Pete Richard. They will witness the decisive naval battle at Midway. Scott is given command of the hapless carrier *Franklin*. In never before shown Navy footage, the audience can view the desperate Kamikaze attacks which nearly destroy his ship. Now an admiral, Scott looks proudly back on all these historic events as he leaves his last command for retirement. Jet fighters fly overhead as if to signal the Navy's future.

This movie has a most interesting and colorful production history. Before resumption of the filming in 1948, Producer Jerry Wald and Director Delmer Daves culled through over 4 million feet of Navy footage and picked out about 2200 feet for *Task Force*. They unearthed footage of the *Langley* and the *Saratoga* during their early years of service. Many of these old clips were from the silent movie era and had to be sped up by an optical process of from 16 frames per second to twenty-four. The very

spectacular color footage of Kamikaze attacks off Okinawa were also shown in the picture. Wald decided he would make the film half black and white and the rest in color in order to integrate the earlier clips with the more recent color ones. By using the early *Langley* and *Saratoga* footage, he could obviate the need for the less credible miniatures of the two older carriers. Stunt pilot Paul Mantz offered his expertise and talents once again to Warner Bros. It was Mantz who found the old de Haviland and Helldiver aircraft that added so much to the earlier carrier sequences. He also flew the old VE-7 in the 1923 clip.

The film company spent twenty-four days aboard the *Essex* class carrier *Antietam* off the coast of California. On board were 117 actors and technicians and over a hundred tons of studio equipment. Certain restrictions were imposed on the movie company while the carrier continued its normal operations. In order to avoid unnecessary saluting, actors in uniform were asked not to wear their hats. The Navy requested they wear coats and ties at dinner and wait for the executive office before sitting. The studio was told that "extras" were forbidden on the flight deck during operations. Warner Bros. would have to notify the Actor's Guild that only ships personnel were to be used in background shots.[4] During all these days at sea, the *Antietam* played the role of the *Saratoga*, the *Yorktown*, the *Hornet*, and the *Franklin*. The baby escort carrier USS *Bairoko* was used in enhancing the *Langley* sequences.

Along with the usual sea-sickness, the film makers had some trying moments while shooting the film. During target practice, a target burst into flames and headed toward the bridge where Gary Cooper and others were watching the shooting. Luckily, it veered off and splashed into the water, thereby giving everybody a sample of what a Kamikaze attack may have been like. In another unexpected event in making the movie, Gary Cooper was marooned in an admiral's gig when its engine conked out in the fog off Long Beach, California. The gig which was carrying civilian-clothed Gary Cooper to an admiral's retirement on-shore was finally towed to a landing without mishap.[5] All these unusual incidents did not deter Cooper and his wife from celebrating their fifteenth anniversary during the film's production.

3. Letter from Wm. Guthrie to Capt. E. M. Eller, August 19, 1948, *Task Force*, Production Papers, Warner Bros. Archives, U.S.C.

4. Memo from Phil Freedman to Wm. L. Guthrie, Oct. 8, 1948, *Task Force*, Production Notes, Warner Bros. Archives, U.S.C.

5. *Ibid.*, n.d.

MIDWAY

Two more movies about the role of American aircraft carriers in the Pacific War were released by Hollywood studios during the Korean War and Cold War periods of the 1950s. They were *Flat Top* in 1952 and *Battle Stations* in 1956. Both films were neither money-makers nor exceptional. In the 1960s there was a paucity of war films partly due to the unpopularity of the Vietnam War. When Fox's *Tora! Tora! Tora!*, an expensive account of the Pearl Harbor attack did poorly at the box office, it seemed that these kinds of films had their day. Yet in 1975, Producer Walter Mirisch began preparing for his production of *Midway*, the story of America's greatest naval victory in World War II. Mirisch and his investors reasoned that enough time had past to blunt anti-war sentiments of the "Sixties" and to now exploit the patriotic ardor expected with the upcoming Bicentennial celebration.[6] It was believed that a film of this kind could both tap the nostalgic patriotism of Americans who had lived through the Second World War and attract great numbers of teenagers whose interests in gore and seeing old airplanes far surpassed any patriotic inclinations. Knowing that Americans needed a psychological boost after the disaster in Vietnam, it was felt that they were ready to see a film about the great naval battle that turned the tide against Japan. It was hoped that even the Japanese would want to see it along with other Asians. The projections on the film proved correct and *Midway* became the sixth largest grossing film in 1976 and had a successful run in Japan.

The Navy was very interested in cooperating in the making of this film. The upbeat nature of the outcome of the Battle of Midway would be good for recruitment; the film could also serve as an adjunct to the Sea-Air Operation Hall spotlighting carrier operations in the new Air and Space Museum in Washington D.C. Most importantly, unlike *Tora, Tora, Tora* which suggested both American incompetence and the reality of a victorious enemy, *Midway* was a feather in the cap of the Navy. It revealed the brilliance of American naval leadership and the indomitable will of the American fighting man.

For its part, the Navy offered the studio color combat and gun-camera footage and the use of its only remaining World War II carrier, the USS *Lexington*, based at Pensacola, Florida. Mindful that air crashes were hurtful to their image, the Navy prohibited Mirisch and company from using their two rented F4F *Wildcat* fighter aircraft from taking off from the carrier even though they were fully tested.

Some local theaters publicized naval recruitment when they showed *Midway*. A picture of new Navy enlistees being sworn in in front of a local theater in Woburn, Massa-chusetts, was carried by 20 newspapers in the Boston area. Employees in a Lake Charles, Louisiana theater wore uniforms furnished them by the Navy in conjunction of the showing of *Midway*.

Midway finished shooting on July 20, 1975, but was not released until the next summer so it could benefit from and add to the Bicentennial celebration. The first three days of its opening surpassed both *Earthquake* and *Airport*, the big movie winners of 1975.[7]

This motion picture is a fictionalized version of the greatest naval battle fought since Trafalgar, the Battle of Midway, which took place in June 1942. At stake were the remaining units of the Pacific Fleet and with their loss, a possible attack on the American West Coast. Nimitz begins to ready his combined fleet for retaliation. Captain Matt Garth (Charlton Heston), a fictionalized character who is woven into a story with actual American naval officers and Comdr. Joseph Rochefort (Hal Holbrook) are convinced that an enemy attack is imminent, the question is where they will strike. Rochefort breaks the Japanese code and is convinced their objective is Midway, some 900 miles northwest of Hawaii. While the government in Washington thinks an attack on Midway is a ruse, Admiral Nimitz (Henry Fonda) readies his fleet for action anyway. When he finds out that his carrier chief Admiral "Bull" Halsey is in the hospital with a skin infection, he is forced to appoint a new commander for Task Force 16. In a momentous decision, he asks Admiral Raymond Spruance (Glenn Ford) to command the fleet. Though Spruance is not a flyer and has never commanded a carrier, he is the perfect choice.

While preparations are being made for this great naval encounter, Garth is stunned to find out that his fighter pilot son (Edward Albert) is in love with a Japanese-American girl Haruku (Christina Kokubo) whose family is in trouble with the government. Garth pledges to his son that he will help him, but the younger man thinks his father's assignment to the *Yorktown* is only an effort to break up his romance. Father and son are not speaking to each other as the battle begins.

The Japanese plan is to head Admiral Nagumo's (James Shigeta) carrier force towards Midway. The admiral does not know where the deadly American carriers are, but they know where he is. He attacks Midway in preparation for a landing, but fails to knock out the American air strip on the island. In a frenzy of fateful decision-making, he arms his planes for another attack, but rearms them with anti-ship bombs when he hears that the Americans are near. Using every airplane available, the Americans attack the Japanese carriers. Ensign George

6. *New West*, July 5, 1976.

7. Box Office, *Showmandiser*, July 23, 1976.

THE MIRISCH CORPORATION PRESENTS

MIDWAY

In **SENSURROUND**
The sights, sounds and actual sensations of combat. So real you can <u>feel</u> it.

A WALTER MIRISCH PRODUCTION
STARRING
CHARLTON HESTON • HENRY FONDA

GUEST STARS
JAMES COBURN • GLENN FORD • HAL HOLBROOK • TOSHIRO MIFUNE • ROBERT MITCHUM • CLIFF ROBERTSON

ROBERT WAGNER   ALSO STARRING   ROBERT WEBBER • ED NELSON • JAMES SHIGETA   WRITTEN BY   MUSIC BY   DIRECTED BY
CHRISTINA KOKUBO and EDWARD ALBERT   DONALD S. SANFORD • JOHN WILLIAMS • JACK SMIGHT

PRODUCED BY   WALTER MIRISCH   A UNIVERSAL PICTURE • TECHNICOLOR ® PANAVISION ®   [PG] PARENTAL GUIDANCE SUGGESTED
SOME MATERIAL MAY NOT BE SUITABLE FOR PRE-TEENAGERS

THEATRE

During the bicentennial year of 1976, Americans in large numbers were ready to see *Midway*, which depicted the U.S. Navy's decisive victory in June 1942.

Gay (Kevin Dodson) is the only survivor of Torpedo Squadron 8's courageous attack. He witnesses the entire battle in the water and sees the Japanese carriers each being destroyed by American dive bombers. In this encounter, Tom Garth is seriously wounded and burned in the picture's most gruesome scene. The Americans sink three enemy carriers and seek out the fourth. Having been reconciled with his son, Captain Garth leads an attack on the last enemy carrier, the *Hiryu*. He is killed, but the last of the four Japanese carriers and their air crews are destroyed, and so is the valiant American carrier, the *Yorktown*. The Americans victoriously return to Pearl Harbor where Nimitz and Spruance review their successes. Tom Garth is met by Haruku at the pier.

In the last scene of the movie, Nimitz asks code-breaker Rochefort whether he thinks the Americans were better than the Japanese or just luckier. The movie does try to tell us, but the battle sequences are too muddled to get a clear opinion. The United States actually won the Battle of Midway for both reasons. The Americans were enormously lucky to break the Japanese code and to catch Admiral Nagumo while he was changing his bombs. But

deadly American dive bombing and resourceful intelligence capability are more than just luck. Unfortunately, reviewer Arthur Knight may be quite right when he says the film never comes close to answering the question posed by Admiral Nimitz at the close of the picture.[8]

Getting proper military equipment for these kinds of epic war films naturally became more difficult as World War II faded into the past. With the scrapping of ships, combat footage was at a premium. The producers of *Midway* were also able to use out-takes from several different motion pictures and documentaries. These included *Tora, Tora, Tora, Thirty Seconds over Tokyo, Dive Bomber, Flying Leathernecks, Admiral Yamamoto, The Fighting Lady*, and the war-time documentary *The Battle of Midway*. Fortunately, the Navy allowed Mirisch and company to use its last World War II vintage carrier, the *Lexington* at Pensacola. Exterior and interior shots were taken in port. Other footage was shot at sea when 50 actors and craftsmen went on a one week cruise. According to regulations, normal operations were not curtailed. Many of the Hollywood people suffered because their state-

8. *Hollywood Reporter*, p. 2, 9, June 17, 1976.

rooms were just below the take-off pad where flights continued day and night. Much filming took place on Universal Studio's Stage 22 where technicians built a ship out of genuine scrap that was designed to pull apart in combat scenes. This would allow such activities such as back projection and the setting of fires. Several locations in the Los Angeles area were used by the film company including Fort MacArthur, Long Beach Naval Station, the Naval Air Station at Pt. Mugu and the Japanese Gardens in San Marino.[9]

Though Mirisch and company tried to get the best footage possible, they also needed to round up a number of plane types that had seen action at Midway. The one PBY-5A was perfect as it posed as twelve different *Catalinas* in the picture; privately owned FM-2 *Wildcats* were purposely used as stand-ins for the fighter used in the battle as were Japanese "Zeros," "Vals," and "Kates" brought to life again from Fox's *Tora! Tora! Tora!* The studio was also able to borrow a number of non-flyable airplanes for some of the sound stage process shots. They were SBD-5 *Dauntless* dive bombers, another FM-2 *Wildcat* and a SNJ-5 training plane modified to appear as a Douglas TBD *Devastator* torpedo bomber. The number of planes used in combat sequences that were out of character limited the film's authenticity. An example of this was the widely seen crash and splitting apart of a Grumman F6F *Hellcat* on the deck of a carrier when it was returning from a mission. These planes were not flown during the Battle of Midway in June, 1942.

9. *Midway Press Book*, p. 12. Academy of Motion Picture Arts and Sciences, Margaret Herrick Library, Beverly Hills, CA.

Downed Ensign George Gay (Kevin Dodson), the only survivor of Torpedo Squadron 8 gets a close-up view of the battle in Midway.

OPPOSITE PAGE, TOP: In Battle Plot Room at Pearl Harbor Admirals Nimitz (Henry Fonda), Spruance (Glenn Ford) and Halsey (Robert Mitchum) plan the defense of Midway Island.

OPPOSITE PAGE, BOTTOM: In a discussion aboard the aircraft carrier *Akagi* Admirals Kusata (Pat Morita) and Nagumo (James Shigeta) with Cmdr. Genda (Robert Ito), right, discuss their attack plan.

BELOW: Charlton Heston, left, and Anthony Herrera fly their SBD *Dauntless* bomber towards a Japanese carrier.

FLAT TOP

Another film about carrier operations in the Pacific War is also a Mirisch picture. It is entitled *Flat Top*. Released in 1952, this picture and *Battle Stations* are the only other films of this genre made between *Task Force* in 1949 and *Midway* in 1976. Monogram's *Flat Top* is a low-budget film which offers very little that is new or stimulating about carrier warfare. Despite some good Navy footage and the use of the aircraft carrier USS *Princeton* in the production, it is just an earnest but standard depiction of life aboard a carrier in World War II. Fortunately, the *Princeton* which was on its way to a second tour of duty off Korea at the time had a full complement of F4U *Corsair* fighters on board. This lent visual credibility to the story because *Corsairs* were also used in the Second World War.[10]

The story line in *Flat Top* is typical of many war dramas. The film is about an experienced airman and his relationship with his men. As Dan Collier (Sterling Hayden) awaits the landing of his new air group while heading for Korea, he reflects back to 1944 when another group of inexperienced flyers landed on the same ship. A no-nonsense man, who goes by the book, he is angered when one of his new pilots disobeys landing instructions and lands anyway. When the young man is "decked," the group's executive officer Joe Rodgers (Richard Carlson) asks Collier to go easier on the man, but Collier uses the event as an opportunity to show his men that discipline in his outfit is of prime importance. He believes in the Navy's old maxim that it is teamwork and not individual acts that have made the service great. Collier will not talk to his pilots about their fears about the upcoming combat and scolds them for breaking radio silence in their first sortie against the enemy. The conflict widens as Joe Rodgers is not recommended for promotion. The air group does well in battle anyway and most of the men begin to see that Collier's regimen has been correct. Rodger is even endorsed by Collier to become the new group commander when the veteran pilot is ordered to another command. The film does contain some excellent footage of island landings, entire naval task forces, and air-to-air combat between *Corsairs* and *Zeros*.

BATTLE STATIONS

As in the case of *Flat Top*, much of the filming of Columbia Pictures *Battle Stations* was shot on the aircraft carrier *Princeton*. The film crew and actors spent four weeks on this *Essex* class carrier which played the role of her sister ship, the USS *Franklin*, the subject of the movie. The *Princeton* conveniently carried a number of World War II planes. They had a composite squadron aboard which had F4U-4 and -5 *Corsair* fighters and an anti-submarine unit which still flew TBM-3 *Avengers*. Both of these types served in the Pacific in 1945. Using Navy footage, the studio was able to avoid the high cost of miniatures and mock-ups. It delivered an authentic movie to the viewing public.

Previewed at Columbia Pictures on January 27, 1956, this drama about the Battle of Okinawa did not get good reviews. According to some critics the movie was riddled with stereotypical characters. Some writers complained that the script had every service movie cliche imaginable.[11]

Battle Stations is a semi-fictional account of the intrepid carrier *Franklin* which was almost lost to Kamikaze attacks off Okinawa. The central characters in the motion picture are Chaplin McIntyre (John Lund) who narrates the story of death and destruction aboard the carrier. As the ship moves closer towards action, he tries to build character in the enlisted men while also ministering to their needs. Captain Mathers (Richard Boone) is a dedicated officer who works his crew to the bone so that they will be ready for action. Chief "Buck" Fitzpatrick (William Bendix) seems tough on the outside, but is really a gentle man. His protagonist is "Wanabe" Chief Chris Jordan (Keith Brasselle), an angry, resentful man who has been passed over for Chief. Chris hits "Buck" in a fight, but the older man does not report the incident. Ensign Kelly (William Leslie) is a pilot who has been "decked" for insubordination.

The carrier *Franklin* is attacked by Kamikazes as she lay off Okinawa. One of the so-called "bandits" drops two large bombs on the carrier, but does not crash into the big ship. Kelly who has been called back to fly, shoots down the plane and returns to the ship which is both listing and on fire. Chris shows his real mettle when he saves the old Chief from certain death below decks. In true Navy fashion, the captain fights to keep the ship afloat and wins. In the midst of the battle, McIntyre prays and is convinced that the encounter with the enemy has drawn the whole crew closer to faith. Finally, after hours of struggle, the *Franklin* moves out of the combat zone to an anchorage. Chris is ceremoniously promoted to Chief.

10. Bruce W. Orriss, *When Hollywood Ruled the Skies* (Hawthorne: Aero Associates, Inc. 1984), p. 165.

11. *Variety*, February 6, 1956.

6

THE WAR STILL RAGES
World War II Navy Submarine Movies, 1951-1959

Submarine movies have always been popular with American movie-goers. There is something mysterious about these relatively small ships that can surface, dive and attack unexpectedly. A lot of the anger and interest in the submarine is traced to the Imperial German submarine campaigns during the First World War. The sinking of neutral ships without warning was intolerable to the American people. After the war much of the public wanted submarines outlawed along with poison gas. Yet an interest remained, as seen by the great number of books and successful movies about these craft. Motion picture producers were intrigued by the great number of possibilities for using submarine stories because the boats were secretive and in constant danger while on patrol. They saw that the close quarters aboard ship offered movie plots which emphasized relationships between officers and their men and between the men themselves. As early as 1915, just six months before the sinking of *Lusitania*, a film entitled *A Submarine Pilot* appeared. Starring Syd Chaplin, it featured the submarine "above water, submerging, and firing a torpedo . . . and the use of a periscope is (was) also illustrated."[1] The submarine film remained popular after the First World War was over. An important movie during this era was John Ford's silent classic, *Men Without Women* (1930). This fascinating moving picture depicted the agony and death aboard a sunken American underseas craft in Asian waters. Another successful film was Warner Bros.' *Submarine D-1* which featured escape lungs and diving bells, demonstrating the dangers and the appeal of stories set underwater.

Movies about American submarines continued to be produced during the Second World War, but seldom touched on the genuine wartime accomplishments of the "silent service." While U.S. submarines were demolishing the Japanese merchant marine and Navy in the Pacific, *Crash Dive* (1943) features a fictional submarine whose mission it was to destroy a Nazi U-Boat base somewhere in the Atlantic. Another film, *Destination Tokyo* (1943) tells the story about a submarine sortie to Japan for the purpose of collecting weather information for the forthcoming Doolittle Raid on Tokyo.

It was not until the Korean War in the early 1950s that several movies began describing the real submarine war in the Pacific. Between 1951 and 1959, no less than eight feature films about American submarine operations against Japan were made in Hollywood. Appearing at .hat time, a large number of books and television shows also stimulated interest in this topic.

There were a number of reasons for the popularity of the submarine movie during the war against Japan. Women audiences were drawn to these films because they featured handsome actors who played dramatic and heroic submarine commanders. They were further enticed by the addition of romantic sub-plots. Some of the headliners in these motion pictures were John Wayne, William Holden, Clark Gable, Burt Lancaster, Glenn Ford, Ronald Reagan, James Garner, and Edmund O'Brien. Also bringing interest to the whole issue of submarines was a Soviet submarine buildup in the 1950s and the development of the nuclear ballistic missile submarine at the end of the decade.

OPERATION PACIFIC

The Warner Bros. production *Operation Pacific* released in 1951 was the first major post-war film about submarine operations against Japan in the Pacific. Like its war-time predecessor, *Destination Tokyo*, *Operation Pacific* included fictitious stories based on real events. Using the best post-war sources available, Carl Milliken, Jr., Warner's chief researcher investigated all kinds of incidents which could be made into screen plays. As the Cold War heated up, government officials and movie-makers alike felt that the new wave of war movies should both inform and entertain audiences with pictures that stressed professionalism

1. Quoted in Jeanine Basinger, *The World War II Combat Film: Anatomy of a Genre* (New York: Columbia University Press, 1986) pp. 105-6.

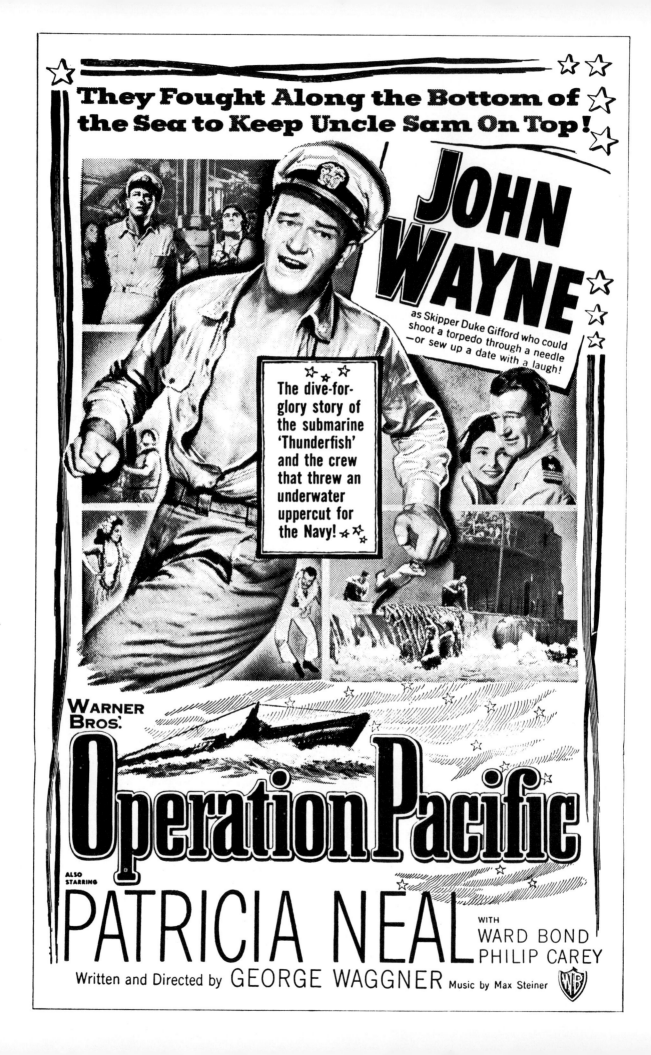

in the military. Collaboration between the military and commercial film companies hit its peak between 1948 and 1962.[2] *Operation Pacific* was one of the first of this kind of movie produced.

Millikin and screenwriter George Waggner examined the record of the underseas service and came away with many stories that would heighten the dramatic action aboard *Operation Pacific's* submarine, the fictional USS *Thunderfish*. One of their findings incorporated in the film was inspired by the USS *Angler's* (SS-240) special mission. In March 1944, the *Angler* was ordered to rescue twenty Americans on the northern coast of Panay. Instead they found 58 eager people waiting to board the sub. With the old submarine adage in mind that "there is no room aboard a submarine for everything but a mistake," all were taken aboard. The twelve-day run to Australia was arduous and claustrophobic as a large percentage of the passengers suffered from tropical ulcers which gave off an unpleasant odor. The film's fictionalized version of this story was toned down. In the movie, the *Thunderfish* picks up two nuns and fifteen or twenty children from an enemy-held island. The children happily run around the boat even when the sub tries to sink a Japanese aircraft carrier; they are much quieter during the vicious depth-charge attack which follows. The courageous nuns and their charges make the trip safely back to Pearl Harbor with the youngest child aboard being fed by an ersatz baby bottle fashioned by the crew.

Another incident gleaned from Navy records and written into the script was the tragic story of Commander Howard Gilmore of the USS *Growler* (SS-215). On the night of April 12, 1943, the *Growler* was attacked by an enemy provision ship while recharging her batteries. Gilmore and a few others were on the bridge when the ships collided. Wounded by enemy gun fire, Gilmore heroically had all hatches closed and ordered his crew to "take her down" without him. Gilmore drifted to his death as the sub dove for safety. He had sacrificed his life to save his ship. The sequence in *Operation Pacific* which tries to emulate the *Growler* incident keeps the same theme of the dedicated captain's sacrifice, but is handled differently. "Pop" Perry (Ward Bond), the skipper is unhappy about the *Thunderfish's* "dud" torpedo shots. He is stunned when he runs into a Japanese freighter that turns out to be a decoy ship (Q-Boat). Surfacing, he is met by gunfire from the enemy ship. As was the case with the *Growler*, Perry orders the sub to submerge and loses his life on the bridge. "Duke" Gifford (John Wayne) takes over the boat and rams the enemy. It should be noted that both of the bows of the *Growler* and the fictional *Thunderfish* are severely damaged. While the Japanese did not use Q-Boats in the war, the real USS *Amberjack*

(SS-219) did have a run-in with a heavily armed enemy munitions ship in early 1943. In this event, machine gun fire did hit the sub's conning tower, wounding an officer in the hand.[3]

Submarine commander Ward Bond seconds before he makes his heroic "take her down" order in Warner Bros. *Operation Pacific.*

A third incident taken from the annals of submarine history and used in *Operation Pacific* was the story of unreliable torpedoes used in the first two years of the war. It appears that American steam driven torpedoes ran at depths below the target's steel hull and that its magnetic detonator did not activate the warhead of the torpedo. Another fault of these torpedoes was that the alternate detonator sometimes jammed when the impact of the target was too direct or severe. "Dud" torpedoes were dispiriting to crews as well as being dangerous to their safety. At the end of 1943, some remedies for torpedo failure were put in place with the standard torpedo exploding true when aimed true.[4] A problem torpedo sequence was written into the script of *Operation Pacific*, but a few senior

2. Russel E. Shane, *An Analysis of Motion Pictures about War Released by the American Film Industry* (New York: Arnio Press, 1976), p. 93.

3. Theodore Roscoe, *United States Submarine Operations in World War II* (Annapolis: Naval Institute Press, 1949), p. 218.

4. Kenneth J. Hagan, *The People's Navy* (New York: The Free Press, 1991), p. 329.

officers wanted this segment removed because they felt it would bring discredit to the Navy and was "like dragging a dead cat a long ways."[5] However, Admiral Charles A. Lockwood (Ret.), the film's Technical Advisor and studio executives held firm and the depiction of the torpedo failures was not deleted from the picture. In the movie's torpedo sequence, the *Thunderfish* is denied a sure kill of an enemy carrier when its torpedo fails to explode on target. "Duke" Gifford, now commanding is assigned to find out why. In a show of American "know how" and the inherent cleverness of a Navy Chief Petty Officer (Jack Pennick), they correct the problem by placing a lighter aluminum firing pin in the torpedo and to everyone's delight it works.

A gala joint premier of *Operation Pacific* was held in both Hollywood, California at the Warner's Hollywood Theater and at the New London Submarine Base in Connecticut on January 9, 1951. The premiers occurred just six months after hostilities in Korea broke out and reverberated with patriotism. In Hollywood, there was a parade featuring the 60 piece Naval Training Center Band from San Diego; Navy Waves delivered tickets to movie columnists and Hollywood stars in Navy jeeps. A Navy blimp towing a streamer reading *Operation Pacific* flew over the city; all Navy patrol and mobile units were ordered to carry *Operation Pacific* banners while shore-patrol units helped police keep order. Some of Hollywood's top performers including Lucille Ball and Ronald Reagan attended. A large number of high ranking officers from all branches of the service were invited and no less than 23 admirals were in attendance. Singing star Gordon MacRae acted as Master of Ceremonies.[6]

Another premier took place simultaneously at the New London Submarine Base. The base was opened to the public as special trains from New York City and Boston brought newsmen to cover the festivities. Other promotional ideas for advancing the film were Warner Bros. brochures sent to schools and libraries to encourage enlistments in the Navy.

The film *Operation Pacific* is really two separate stories fastened together about the military and personal life of a World War II submarine officer, "Duke" Gifford (John Wayne). Gifford is skipper "pop" Perry's (Ward Bond) executive officer on the submarine *Thunderfish*. Perry tries to bring Gifford and Mary Stuart (Patricia Neal), Gifford's divorced wife and now a nurse at Pearl Harbor back together again. Perry's younger brother (Philip Carey), a Navy flyer, makes a play for Mary, but she still loves Gifford. When the *Thunderfish* goes to sea, many of its torpedoes fail to perform and don't destroy enemy shipping. After one such failure, Perry is gunned down by a Japanese freighter and is killed. Gifford is forced to leave Perry top-side when he dives to save the ship. Back at Pearl Harbor, Perry's brother falsely accuses Gifford for causing his brother's death. Mary tries to console Gifford, but they argue. Gifford and his crew are assigned to correct the torpedo problem and they do. The *Thunderfish* is sent out on another patrol and finds itself right in the middle of a large Japanese task force. After the sub sends a message to U.S. naval headquarters warning them of enemy movements, a fierce battle ensues and the *Thun-*

5. *Hollywood Citizen News*, January 8, 1951.

6. Production File, *Operation Pacific, Press Summary, folder 3657.* Warner Bros. Archives, U.S.C.

The sub's "exec" John Wayne takes over after the captain's death as young Ensign Martin Milner looks on.

derfish sinks a lot of Japanese warships. Gifford then picks up a downed American pilot who turns out to be Bob Perry. The latter now recognizes that he has been wrong about accusing Gifford for his brother's death and they make up. Back at Pearl Harbor, Mary waits for Gifford and they are finally reconciled.

Operation Pacific was one of the most technically advanced movies ever made in Hollywood. Under the supervision of Art Director Leo Kutter and Technical Advisor Admiral Charles A. Lockwood, the studio built a life-size replica of a fleet submarine. Except for the stern which had to be shortened, it was perfect. Kutter insisted that the replica of the *Copperfin* which he had built for *Destination Tokyo* could not be used because it did not match the story action of *Operation Pacific*. Cut-up backdrops of submarines built to a smaller scale were placed in the background in order to give the illusion of distance. Little boys and midgets fitted in Navy uniforms were used to "man" those "boats." A 623,000 gallon water tank was put in place while the largest piece of muslin ever rigged on a sound stage was used to surround the full-scale submarine with complete sky-backing. An eight-man gun crew from the submarine *Sawfish* (SS-276) was sent to the studio from Terminal Island to fire the guns on the set and instruct the actors.[7] The studio also developed a revolutionary type of underwater motor which turned a four-bladed propeller to simulate white water conditions or extreme turbulence. Everything was so authentic that Admiral Lockwood told people on the set that he was home-sick.

SUBMARINE COMMAND

Paramount's *Submarine Command* was produced shortly after *Operation Pacific*. It was reviewed in *Variety Daily* on June 21, 1951. Like the Warner Bros. film, Paramount employed a renowned submarine expert as the film's technical advisor. As producer of the dynamic television series *The Silent Service*, Rear Admiral Thomas Dykers had a great deal of experience with submarines. His exploits during the war as skipper of the successful USS *Jack* (SS-259) helped insure the credibility of the production.

Submarine Command's theme revolves around a fateful decision made by executive officer Ken White (William Holden) on the last day of World War II. As the *Tigerfish* is attacked by enemy aircraft, White orders the sub to crash dive even though the skipper Comdr. Rice (Jack Gregson) and another man are still on the bridge and will be killed. Though he saves the ship, he earns the boundless contempt of Chief Boyer (William

Bendix). White becomes full of self-doubt even though Rice's wife and father don't blame him for the death. After the war, the trauma persists and threatens to wreck his marriage. Bored with a desk job, he thinks seriously of quitting the Navy.

He is given command of the *Tigershark* when it is taken out of moth-balls and readied for service in Korea. He is again faced with the disapproval of Chief Boyer who is assigned to the same ship and reminds him of that fateful decision made on the last day of the war. Ken's chance to rid himself of self-doubt comes when he is assigned to an important mission to rescue 400 Americans held on the Korean Coast. Ken takes the *Tigershark* through a minefield in the range of shore batteries. "The odds are right this time—a sub for 400 people," exults Ken. Though the sub is sunk, the mission is accomplished and Ken is greeted as a hero. He wins the approval of Boyer and with his new found self-respect, he returns to his wife with plans to make a go of their marriage.

The movie was shot around San Diego and Mare Island, California. William Holden and the Paramount unit spent several days making submarine runs and location spotting near San Diego. Practice runs in two subs were made; one of them submerged and Holden got a chance to use the periscope. For two hours, the film company shot the picture's opening sequence of a single Japanese airplane attack on the submarine not far from residential neighborhoods. A military alert named "Operation Meatball" was called to keep the filming area clear. The plane that was used was a repainted F8F *Bearcat*. Excellent footage from Mare Island's submarine base was used showing base activities as well as a large number of fleet type submarines in mothballs.

TORPEDO ALLEY

Allied Artist's *Torpedo Alley* is yet another submarine film that came out during the Korean War. Completed on July 23, 1952, it began its run shortly after *Submarine Command* hit the marquees. Like *Submarine Command* it spans the period from the end of World War II through the Korean War. Just as the hero in *Submarine Command* is agonized because he left the skipper on the bridge in a dive for safety, pilot Bob Bingham (Mark Stevens) in *Torpedo Alley* is devastated believing that he was responsible for the death of two of his air crew members. Both men had developed guilt complexes though they are never reproached for their actions. The wartime accident bedevils Bingham in civilian life and he fails to adjust.

7. *Variety*, September 29, 1950.

William Bendix shows his skill with the accordian in Paramount's *Submarine Command.*

Impressed by the submarine crew that picked him up during the war, he re-enlists in the Navy and asks for submarine duty. At the Navy sub school in New London, he meets many of the officers he befriended when he was picked up by the submarine *Stingray* during the war. He also falls in love with nurse Susan Peabody (Dorothy Malone) who is the steady girlfriend of his buddy Lt. Gates (Douglas Kennedy). Gates is not strongly committed to the nurse and so there is not a lot of squabbling for her hand. When the Korean War breaks out Bingham, Gates, and the old skipper ship out to Korea in a recommissioned submarine. Bingham becomes a hero on this trip and now is able to shed his guilt. He had saved the sub by controlling a dangerous fire on board and with a small contingent of men he leads an attack on a North Korean railroad tunnel on the coast. When he is wounded, he is placed on a hospital ship where he is cared for by his love, Susan. His buddy Gates is on the ship too, but his hurt feelings because of Susan's defection is quickly assuaged when he casts his eyes on another nurse.

This picture was made at the sub base at New London, San Diego Naval Training Center, and at sea. The film's strongest attribute is its informative narrative. Like a documentary, it skillfully tells the audience about submarines. For example, we learn from the dialogue that a fleet submarine has a crew of 85 and costs $12,000,000. Most interesting was the detailed footage of the submarine training facilities at New London.[8]

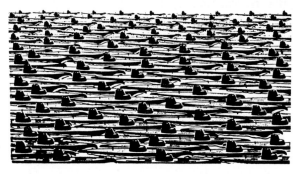

HOW MANY SUBS IN THIS PICTURE?
★ ★ ★ ★ ★ ★ ★
"Torpedo Alley" Contest Mat FREE!
USE IT IN NEWSPAPERS AND IN YOUR HERALDS!

HOW MANY SUBMARINES IN THIS PICTURE? Here's a contest that will have the whole town guessing . . . and talking about "Torpedo Alley." Offer ticket prizes to those submitting correct answers. Plant the picture puzzle with your newspaper editor, or print it in your theatre program. If you're too busy with your "Torpedo Alley" campaign to count the number of subs yourself, the correct answer is 63.
Order Contest Mat from Exploitation Dept., Allied Artists

8. *New York Times*, December 20, 1952.

DEADLIEST UNDERSEA CORRIDOR IN THE WORLD!

Periscope patrol...stabbing its torpedoes into the very jaws of the Korean sub trap!

MARK STEVENS in *Torpedo Alley*

AN ALLIED ARTISTS PICTURE

Filmed with The Cooperation of The U. S. NAVY

co-starring DOROTHY MALONE · CHARLES WINNINGER · BILL WILLIAMS
with Douglas Kennedy

Her lips moored fast the toughest torpedo-man afloat!

A LINDSLEY PARSONS PRODUCTION   ASSOCIATE PRODUCER John H. Burrows   DIRECTED BY Lew Landers   WRITTEN BY Sam Roeca and Warren Douglas

HELLCATS OF THE NAVY

It was not until 1957 that another submarine picture would appear. The movie *Hellcats of the Navy* from Columbia Studio got its name from a special submarine attack group which successfully entered the Sea of Japan in early 1945. Based on a book by Admiral Charles A. Lockwood, the coordinator of that operation, nine American submarines entered Japanese waters after their sonar equipment had been adjusted to deal with the minefields which had effectively blocked their entrance to this protected zone. Once into this "hunting ground," over 70,000 tons of shipping were quickly sent to the bottom. Fleet Admiral Chester Nimitz lends credibility to the movie when in the film's forward he states that it was the selfless courage and skill of the Hellcats that opened Japan's last safe shipping lane to attack. *Hellcats of the Navy* is a fictionalized account of these operations. This dramatic story which was previewed on April 4, 1957, begins when Comdr. Casey Abbott (Ronald Reagan), skipper of the submarine *Starfish* is ordered to retrieve a few enemy mines for study. The sub positions itself off the Straits of Tsushima and sends five frogmen to haul in the mines. Abbott, however, is forced to dive precipitously when an enemy ship appears and one of the frogmen, Barton (Harry Lauter) is left behind. Executive officer Landon (Arthur Franz) and others suspect that Abbott's hurried dive occurred because he and Barton were in competition for the same woman. The truth is that Helen (Nancy Davis) did have a brief fling with Barton, but that was only because Abbott wanted to postpone marriage until after the war was over.

The old command dilemma occurs again when Abbott is forced to leave a man at an island radar station when he fails to return to the sub in time. The *Starfish* is sunk during this hard and arduous duty. Abbott, Landon, and a few others amazingly survive still unhappy at what they had to do. Exonerated of any wrong-doing, he enters the Sea of Japan in the *Searay*, his new command, to chart the enemy minefields. The *Searay*'s rudder breaks down as she enters dangerous waters. Abbott leaves the boat to make the needed repairs as the only qualified man to do the job. When a Japanese warship appears, it is Landon who now has to make the fateful decision of whether to dive or not. Landon reasons that it is his duty to dive. But luckily, the enemy ship is sunk and Abbott is picked up. Landon can now see more clearly what the responsibilities of command are and is recommended for command of his own boat. Abbott, free from any false accusations, returns to Helen.

Columbia Pictures publicity people and the Navy promoted the movie in a familiar way. Simultaneous showings of it were presented at both San Diego and New London. The guests in San Diego cruised in a submarine for three hours and then attended a cocktail party at the Officers Club. Visitors in New London were also invited for a three hour cruise which included practice dives on Long Island Sound. That morning, journalists and others attended the recommissioning ceremony for the USS *Cravelle* (SS 292). This submarine took part in that same Sea of Japan offensive during World War II.[9]

9. *Motion Picture Herald*, April 20, 1957.

RUN SILENT, RUN DEEP

Run Silent, Run Deep, United Artist's entry into the submarine movie competition was acclaimed as the best submarine picture ever made. Based on Commander Edward L. Beach's best selling novel, the story was purchased for $50,000 and a percentage of the gross. It may be asked why Bowsley Crowthers, *New York Times* movie critic, wrote that this movie had "the hard, cold ring of truth?"[10] It is not true that four American submarines were sunk off the Bungo Straits nor is there anything to the tale that an American sub hit a Japanese destroyer with a head-on bow torpedo shot. The film's veracity is the result of the absence of the usual stereotypical characters found in these kinds of movies. Not present is the "know-it-all" chief or naive and bungling ensign. Instead, real people emerge. There is the disgruntled officer Cartwright (Brad Dexter) and the skipper's intensely loyal orderly Mueller (Jack Warden). Don Rickles plays a cynical crewman with a great sense of humor. Both the skipper Commander Richardson (Clark Gable) and his "exec" Lt. Bledsoe (Burt Lancaster) are extremely believable as submarine officers. Most importantly, the film is not mired down by the usual contrived romantic angle. It is an all-male film with the exception of an early scene in which Richardson is established as a normal husband married to wife Laura (Mary La Roche).

Run Silent, Run Deep was completed in March, 1958 and was released locally in the Los Angeles area on April 2, the same year. The film was first seen by Navy officials and newspaper men on board the *USS Perch* (SS-313) where it was shown shortly after the sub completed a dive. They were commemorating the 58th anniversary of "Silent Service."[11]

Tension permeates the entire story. The strain is not only the result of fighting a difficult war, but it is also because of the rift between the skipper (Clark Gable) and his "exec" (Burt Lancaster) over who should command. Comdr. Richardson is a vengeful warrior who dreams about destroying a Japanese destroyer nicknamed "Bungo Pete" that had sank his last boat. After a year of desk work, he finally gets another command, but has to "bump" Bledsoe down to "exec." The crew prefers Bledsoe and is confused by Richardson's incessant drilling and seeming cowardice. They do not know why he avoids a Japanese sub on the way to the Bungo Straits. They don't know that Richardson is determined to return to the Straits to finish off the enemy destroyer that had sunk so many American submarines. There is even talk of a mutiny, but Bledsoe is too honorable of an officer to let that happen. There is a severe depth-charge attack when the sub arrives near the Straits. When the skipper

is wounded, Bledsoe takes command and prepares to return to Pearl Harbor. But he changes his mind when he hears that his sub is reported lost by the enemy. He vows to continue the hunt for the hated destroyer. The surprise element in the movie is that "Bungo Pete" is not a destroyer after all, but a Japanese submarine. In a savage combat finale, the subs fight it out and the Americans win. Richardson finally earns the respect of the crew, but is killed in an enemy air strike. Richardson is buried at sea and the ship heads home with the men knowing that their skipper was a true submariner in every sense of the word.

The Navy was both friendly and cooperative with the production company on this movie. It loaned United Artists over $500,000 worth of instruments so that the "mock" or "dummy" ones were not needed. The film staff spent many days at sea on submarines operating out of San Diego. Some of the best miniatures ever made were designed by studio technicians. Powered by in-board motors, underwater shots were done at the studio, and exterior shots were made in the Salton Sea in California. A three-way endless wire rig coordinated, for example, a destroyer miniature coming straight into the camera as torpedoes left from under camera and then exploded on contact.

10. *New York Times*, March 28, 1958.
11. *Los Angeles Times*, April 1, 1958.

There is tension and conflict in *Run Silent, Run Deep* between executive officer Burt Lancaster and captain Clark Gable. Some reviewers believed it to be the best of the submarine films.

TORPEDO RUN

Just a little more than six months after *Run Silent, Run Deep* appeared, yet another submarine drama was released. On October 16, 1958, a special showing of Metro-Goldwyn-Mayer's *Torpedo Run* was seen at the Academy Awards Theater in Los Angeles. It was attended by a large contingent of naval officers, including 12 admirals and 75 captains. The theater was decorated with signal flags and displayed prominently two submarine models. Klieg lights illuminated the intersection of Melrose Avenue and Doheny Drive as naval and film notables entered the theater. Praising the submarine service, the film's program read: "First it was the battleship that ruled the sea lanes. Now the submarine has challenged the imagination of the world, initiating a new era in naval history."[12] This assertion reflected the fear of the Soviet Union's growing submarine force and the need for a sea-based deterrent. Nuclear attack submarines (SSN) and nuclear ballistic submarines (SSBN) were to become the leading force in the Navy's future. Interest in this film was great and a Chief of Information (Chinfo) bulletin directed all commandants to promote it.

Released in 1958, MGM's *Torpedo Run* starred Glenn Ford and Ernest Borgnine. The movie begins in the Philippines at the beginning of the war. Comdr. Barney Doyle (Glenn Ford) is the skipper of the submarine *Grayfish*. Complicating circumstances make his cruise extremely tortuous. This is because his wife and child having been rounded up in the Philippines are being sent to Japan for internment on a large transport ship carrying 1,200 American prisoners. The transport is also acting as a screen protecting the aircraft carrier *Shinaru*. Doyle is horrified to learn his loved ones are on the ship he must sink in order to get at the aircraft carrier. After confiding with his "exec" Lt. Sloane (Ernest Borgnine), he decides to attack the transport. In defending his actions, he tells Sloane they have to do it because "that's what we're here for." If that is not emotionally draining enough, he sinks the transport and then misses the carrier. To make matters worse, he can't pick up any of the American prisoners (his wife and child included) because enemy destroyers are waiting to blow him out of the water. Furious at the loss of family, he takes the *Grayfish* into Tokyo Bay to get another chance at the *Shinaru*. In order to convince the enemy that his sub has been sunk, he shoots out several sailors who died earlier in a depth-charging. The Japanese fall for the ruse and hold back on their fire. Using a torpedo to put a hole in the harbor nets, he makes his move and gets out of the harbor safely. He then gets orders to move into northern waters. Off Kiska, Doyle spots the *Shinaru* lying at an-

chor. The carrier is torpedoed and sunk, but the *Greyfish* is also sunk by the carrier's escorts. Most of the crew are saved because of the successful use of Monsen lungs. They are picked up by another American submarine and are taken back to Pearl Harbor. A colorful refrain of *Anchors Aweigh* is heard in the background.

12. *Hollywood Citizen News*, October 16, 1958.

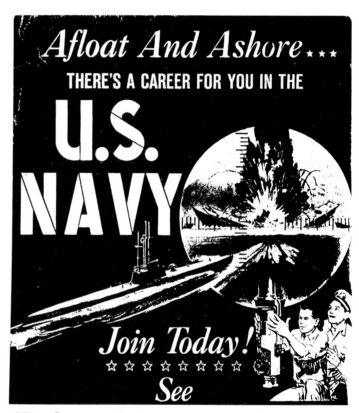

The Greatest Submarine Picture Ever Made
GLENN · ERNEST
FORD BORGNINE

Somewhere out there in the path of peril...is the woman that one of them loves!

M-G-M presents

TORPEDO RUN

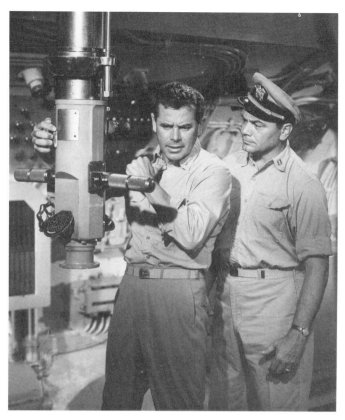

LEFT: Intense anguish is conveyed by Glenn Ford as he prepares to torpedo an enemy transport carrying his loved ones.

BELOW: Depth-charge damage agonizes the crew of the *Greyfish* in MGM's *Torpedo Run*.

UP PERISCOPE

The last of the long cycle of dramatic submarine movies to appear on the screen was Warner's *Up Periscope*, released in early 1959. The writers of this film had to be particularly creative because many submarine story plots had already been explored in earlier movies. There had been plenty of air and depth-charge attacks; men had to be left topside when the sub had to dive; there had been the usual love stories before or between war patrols; misunderstandings between the captain and the crew were seen a number of times. While *Up Periscope* repeats some of these same themes, it still has some novel ideas of its own. There is a love story, but it is at the very beginning of the picture. Thus, Lt (J.G.) Ken Braden (James Garner) has a unique kind of affair with Sally Johnson (Andra Martin). She works for Naval Intelligence as an agent whose job it is to select the best man for an important secret mission. She selects Braden and falls for him. In the middle of the film, there is a brief flashback of the relationship. They will meet again after his heroic action at the end of the film. The audience is introduced to some unusual characters not seen in these kinds of movies before. For example, Alan Hale does not play the stereotypically dull ensign seen over and over again. As Ens. Malone, he is a humorous, good-natured lady's man (he has three Hawaiian girls waiting for him in port) who finally gets a promotion after fifteen years. Comdr. Stevenson (Edmund O'Brien) plays a rather high strung captain of a submarine who goes by the book, but shows flexibility connected with frogman Braden's race to get back to the submarine before the captain has to leave enemy waters because of a dwindling oxygen supply.

This Warner Lakeside Production was previewed at the studio on January 27, 1959. There is much more action than romance in this movie. Braden (Garner) is a highly trained and qualified demolition expert on the submarine *Barracuda*. As the sub pulls out to sea, the skipper tells Braden he will be landing on a tiny island of Kusaie to photograph a Japanese code book. Thousands of American lives will be saved if the code book helps to intercept enemy messages during the impending invasion of the Gilbert and Marshall Islands. Ken Braden and the captain disagree on how close the sub should approach the island. Ken feels his mission is doomed if the sub does not come into the island's lagoon. The sub is attacked by an enemy plane and its wounded executive officer gives the familiar order to "take her down." The dive saves the *Barracuda* and Braden successfully makes some urgent repairs beneath the water line. To the delight of the crew, the *Barracuda* sinks a Japanese destroyer with a well-directed hit. Stevenson surprises Braden when he brings the sub within 500 yards of shore. Braden will have 18 hours to complete his mission or be left behind. His plan is to divert enemy attention by blowing up a wharf as he slips into the radio shack and photographs the Japanese code book. Braden then snakes his way to the water, code in hand. As the sub's oxygen supply is almost depleted, Braden hears metal taps directing him to the sub. Not a minute too soon, they leave the island. The *Barracuda* ties up at Pearl Harbor and receives a warm welcome. Among those cheering in the crowd is Sally

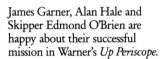

James Garner, Alan Hale and Skipper Edmond O'Brien are happy about their successful mission in Warner's *Up Periscope*.

Johnson.

Up Periscope was made during a time of keen competition for the action-adventure market. It was one of five submarine pictures, including *The Enemy Below* that was made within a period of two years. Not to be outdone, Warner Bros. budgeted the film for $3,000,000. The studio offered actor Ralph Bellamy $25,000 for just a bit part. The movie was filmed at a number of locations. They worked for two weeks on a Navy tug and the submarine *USS Tilefish* (SS-307) at sea and shot beach scenes near Santa Barbara, California. Underwater scenes with James Garner doing his own "frogging" were done in a special water-tank on the Warner lot. The tropical jungle shots were done on Warner's back-lot.[13]

The submarine scenes were dramatically authentic. The exactness of the production was enhanced by building exact replicas of the submarine's conning tower, torpedo room and mess hall. The conning tower, for example, which was placed on a high tank in a sound stage allowed the director to film close-ups of the machine-gunning of the executive officer at the same time the submarine was forced to dive for safety.

The promotion of the picture has little in common with the earlier premier extravaganzas like the one for *Operation Pacific*. There were the usual interesting displays at theater openings around the country. The famous Holland submarine, for example was shown at a Jersey City theater. But the studio's main publicity strategy was to capitalize on the popularity of James Garner. With his current characterization of Bret Maverick fresh in the minds of audiences, it was felt that personal appearances were the best way to sell the film. He did extremely well in places like Texas where he was almost mobbed.

OPERATION PETTICOAT

The last film of the 1950s about submarines was the very successful comedy *Operation Petticoat*. It was previewed at the Village Theater in Westwood on September 22, 1959, and became the third highest grossing film of that year. Despite the film's zany theme about the adventures of a pink American submarine operating in the Pacific during World War II, the Navy apparently felt kindly toward it. According to Producer Robert Arthur, "We blushed when we asked for it (cooperation) and almost fainted when they said OK."[14] Many of the incidents portrayed in the movie seem absurd and implausible. Yet the film is a composite of a number of events that really happened. As in the case of *Destination Tokyo and Operation Pacific*, the film writers searched naval sources for interesting submarine episodes. They were, however, less interested in finding dramatic or informational themes than they were of comedic possibilities. Thus a U.S. submarine like the films pink submarine the *Sea Tiger* did actually exist. Records show that the USS *Seadragon* (SS-194) carried a bright red coat of paint after an explosion blistered her surface paint. The sub first appeared mottled, but was later reduced to her primer coat. This fact was actually noted by Tokyo Rose. The *Sea Tiger*, on the other hand, was pink because supplies were short after she was sunk and a regulation paint job was not possible. When the white primer ran out, the only other paint available was red. The *Sea Tiger's* bureaucratic hassle over the requisitioning of toilet paper actually occurred aboard the real submarine USS *Skipjack* (SS-184). In the movie, Commander Sherman (Cary Grant) skipper of *Sea Tiger* had to take five nurses with them as they headed for Australia. The evacuation by submarine of nurses, women and sometimes children was not uncommon during the early days of the war. Two women actually gave birth aboard the USS *Gato* (SS-212). Finally the film sequence in which Sherman fires a torpedo striking a beached tank is not entirely out of line either. In a gunnery accident aboard the USS *Bowfin* (SS-287), a torpedo from the sub actually struck a bus carrying Japanese sailors.[15]

Operation Petticoat as a service comedy moves beyond the purely slap-stick era to the level of sophisticated wit. Commander Sherman (Cary Grant) and Lt. (J.G.) Holden (Tony Curtis) are the film's leading characters. Sherman, a dedicated officer, wants to repair his boat quickly and get into the fight. Holden, on the other hand, does not really care about the war. He had only become a naval officer in order to impress his rich fiancee. He is a born hustler and Sherman only puts up with him because of his unusual gift of being able to gather up supplies for the sub.

The submarine's chances, once having been sunk, of getting to Australia are not very good. Even a native witch-doctor hired by Holden to bless the voyage admits he is dubious about the outcome. Underway, the submarine amusingly expels black smoke and makes strange noises. Holden further complicates the life of the skipper when he brings five lovely nurses who were marooned on an island aboard the *Sea Tiger*. The film quickly moves from the conflict between the skipper and Holden to a more physical kind of comedy involving the nurses' adjustment to life aboard a submarine. For example, how can a buxom nurse move about in the sub's

13. Production Notes, *Up Periscope*, Warner Bros. Archives, U.S.C.
14. *Los Angeles Mirror-News*, February 23, 1959.
15. *The Hollywood Reporter*, September 28, 1959.

narrow corridors without bringing direct contact with the crew? Director Blake Edwards compounds the problem by designing the corridors four inches narrower than on a real submarine. The head-nurse (Virginia Gregg), a former farm girl who knows mechanics, helps Chief Tostin (Arthur O'Connell) keep the boat afloat by utilizing her girdle and they begin to like each other. Grant as the skipper underplays his part with humor and expression and gets a lot of laughs without saying much. He remains calm even after two Filipino families are taken aboard with their goat. When Tokyo Rose reports that a pink submarine is operating somewhere in the war zone, a mistrustful U.S. Navy goes on the alert to get it. Meanwhile the very attractive, yet extremely clumsy nurse Crandall (Joan O'Brien) gets in Sherman's way as he is about to fire a torpedo at a docked enemy tanker. The torpedo misses the ship and hits a beached armored tank instead. At the same time, another pretty lady, nurse Duran (Dina Merrill) seems to be hitting it off well with Holden until the young officer tells her he is already engaged to a girl back home. The climax of the movie is when an American destroyer spots the *Sea Tiger* and begins a depth-charging barrage. The submarine's fate seems hopeless until Sherman cleverly jettisons the nurses underwear through his torpedo tubes. When the destroyer captain gets a look at nurse Crandall's bra, he cries "the Japanese have nothing like this" and orders a cease fire.   The sub is saved and will get to Australia. While the movie begins with Sherman (now an admiral) reliving his adventures via his log-book of the

soon to be decommissioned submarine *Sea Tiger*, the audience is treated to one more laugh. Holden, now a captain ready to take command of a new nuclear submarine and his wife, the former nurse Duran arrive at the dock to see the old sub. Meanwhile, Sherman, waiting for his wife, watches the accident-prone former nurse Crandall have one last mishap as she crashes the admiral's car while coming to pick him up at the pier.

A good portion of the film *Operation Petticoat* was filmed in Key West, Florida, just a hundred yards away from President Truman's "Little White House" at the naval station. Navy cooperation with the film company stipulated that their help would not cost the taxpayers a penny. The submarine USS *Baloa* (SS-285), a veteran of ten wartime patrols and the destruction of 57,000 tons of enemy shipping was on hand, to work with the studio. Navy personnel were detached long enough to bathe the sub in pink vinyl anti-corrosive paint which was paid for by the studio. Sailors on other submarines got the giggles when they saw the pink *Baloa*. Sailors on the *Baloa* showed they could take a joke and dyed their hats pink to match the sub. The crew was called back after the film was completed to restore the sub to regulation grey.[16]

For interior scenes, Universal-International built a complete replica of a submarine. They cleverly constructed submarine sections that could be removed any time so as to permit the use of cameras almost anywhere in the crowded confines of the warship. This replica actually covered three full sound stages.

16. *Los Angeles Mirror-News*, February 23, 1959.

The Academy of Motion Picture Arts and Sciences

presents for its members

a Special Screening of

OPERATION PETTICOAT

A Granart Production
A Universal-International Release

Sunday, *November 22, 1959 • 8:30 P.M.*

Academy Award Theatre
9038 Melrose Avenue, Hollywood 46, California
CRestview 5-1146

Admission by Academy Membership Card only.
Card must be presented in person by member who may be accompanied by only one guest.

LEFT: Cary Grant and Joan O'Brien meet in a narrow submarine corridor in *Operation Petticoat*.

BELOW: Cary Grant talks to two Navy divers on the set.

RIGHT: The men of the *Sea Tiger* are given a sumptuous meal on the sub's deck hosted by Skipper Cary Grant.

BELOW: Cary Grant relies on Tony Curtis to keep the sub well supplied. Eventually, the crafty junior officer will marry nurse Dina Merrill and command a nuclear submarine.

$\boxed{7}$

THE WAR STILL RAGES

Classic Sea Stories of the 1950s

Both *The Caine Mutiny* (1954) and *Mr. Roberts* (1955) are film classics about the United States Navy in the Second World War. *The Caine Mutiny* is based on the Pulitzer winning novel by Herman Wouk; *Mr. Roberts* is based on a highly successful Broadway play. These two movies are not like the typical wartime Navy feature films with their idealized patriotism and shallowness. Some producers with almost a decade of hindsight now felt that they could develop deeper, more critical themes without upsetting the confidence the American people had won as a result of the war.

THE CAINE MUTINY

The Caine Mutiny had been a stunning literary success and one of the truly great sea stories of the century. It remained on the best-seller list for over two years and was printed in twelve different languages. Its decided pro-Navy slant was powerful enough to run rough-shod over any major criticism during the McCarthy era.[1] It was only natural that several major studios would compete to make the book into a film.

Columbia's Stanley Kramer moved ahead of his competition when he purchased the movie rights from Herman Wouk for $65,000. Getting the production underway, however, was not an easy task. A story about a troubled neurotic captain and the idea of a mutiny was not popular in Navy public relations circles. They believed that the message of the movie would be detrimental to the Navy and did not want it made. Kramer battled the Navy for well over a year and a half for its approval. Naval cooperation and support of a film like this was absolutely essential if the movie were to be successful. Navy ships and bases were needed; by now the public was too sophisticated to accept a movie with unrealistic props and miniatures. There were rumors that the Navy wanted the word "incident" to replace "mutiny" in the title and make the half-crazed Captain Queeg a reserve

Captain Queeg (Humphrey Bogart) begins to show the strain of the trial.

officer instead of an Academy man. Complicating Kramer's efforts was a 37-page outline of a script sent to the Navy from another studio which projected the story as being about a "cornball" Captain Bly with a "Mutiny on the Bounty" thesis. Though this was not an accurate description of either Wouk's book or Stanley Robert's screenplay, it scared some of the men who ran the Navy's public relations office. One admiral said that the picture would make the Navy look like a psycho ward.[2] A group of naval officers headed by Rear Admiral

1. Toronto Film Society, Summer, 1980. *Apocalypse Before*, 1980, p. 1.

2. *Time*, April 7, 1952.

Lewis Parks wanted the script changed to make sure that Queeg and the sloppy crew of the *Caine* were seen by the public as atypical of the U.S. Navy, not an easy task. On the other hand, some officers including Chief of Naval Operations (CNO) Admiral William F. Fechteler liked the book. The stalemate was finally ended when Kramer went over Parks' head and talked directly to the Secretary of the Navy. Parks was ordered to approve Kramer's request for naval cooperation. Captain Walter Karig of the Navy's public relations office later tried to excuse the Navy's footdragging when he said that another studio's submission of an unsatisfactory treatment of the story had caused all the problems and that there was no major difficulty with Kramer's script. Kramer was asked by the Navy, however, to insert a prologue in the film similar to the one in Wouk's book introduction. They wanted him to restate the fact that the story was fictional and that there had never been a mutiny in the United States Navy. Kramer was also asked to write a letter stating the goals of the motion picture. The character of Queeg, however, did not really tarnish the Navy's image. He was not seen as a raving incompetent, but as a battle-weary veteran whose breakdown was caused by the betrayal of his officers.

Columbia President Harry Cohn ordered screenplay writer Stanley Roberts to cut the film to just two hours and he wanted the love story sequence back in the script. Roberts could not stand to delete over fifty pages in the script and quit. Michael Blankfort was hired and both he and Kramer made the necessary cuts in a couple of weeks.[3] The movie became a financial success. The film cost over $3,000,000 to make and grossed between 30 and 35 million dollars.[4]

The Caine Mutiny is a tale about the men of the destroyer-minesweeper *Caine*, a tired old ship which has spent too many months in the war zone. Its new captain is Lt. Commander Phillip Queeg (Humphrey Bogart), a battle-weary veteran of action on the Atlantic. Queeg is a perfectionist and a stickler for detail who annoys his officers and men with his pettiness. While scolding a sailor for wearing his shirt out, Queeg neglects his navigational duties and cuts through his own target line. On another occasion, he shows his cowardice when he prematurely abandons a marine landing craft he is supposed to support. In a bizarre episode, he throws the whole ship into frenzy trying to find out who stole a quart of strawberries from the mess. His officers are very puzzled by this odd behavior. The Executive Officer Lt. Maryk (Van Johnson) is warned by the self-styled "intellectual" Lt. Keefer (Fred MacMurray) that Queeg is exhibiting paranoid tendencies. Keefer is a man of weak character who tries to stay out of trouble while creating

lots of it himself. Maryk, a decent but naive man, begins keeping a medical log of Queeg. Keefer also convinces Willie Keith (Robert Francis), a young and inexperienced ensign that the captain is mentally disturbed. All three officers leave the ship to talk to Admiral Halsey about Queeg's conduct, but Keefer calls it off at the last moment. Queeg's last fiasco is when he does not know what to do when the ship is struck by a typhoon. The ship seems to be foundering and Queeg does nothing. It is at this moment that Maryk decides he must take over the *Caine*. Although this act is not a crime in itself, Maryk will have to explain his conduct to a naval court of inquiry.

After the incident, both Maryk and Keith are called before a naval court. The charges are serious. Keefer, the real instigator of the trouble, was not on the bridge at the time of the takeover and so he is not charged. Little aid and comfort is given to his fellow officers by his testimony. Lt. Barney Greenwald (Jose Ferrer) handles the defense brilliantly by probing into Queeg's personality and uncovering the true nature of Queeg's mental disorder. Queeg's growing nervousness is punctuated by his rolling of steel balls. Queeg almost collapses when Greenwald suggests that he bring in another witness to clarify the strawberry incident. The astonished court brings in a verdict of acquittal.

Later, a slightly drunk Greenwald walks into a noisy victory celebration to tell these officers what he really thinks. He explains that he had to "torpedo" Queeg, an officer with an honorable record, in order to defend Maryk and Keith. He reminds all of them that while they were living the good life as civilians, men like Queeg were doing their dirty work of defending the country and preparing the Navy for war. They had turned their backs on Queeg when he most needed their help. Then Greenwald turns to Keefer and toasts: to the "real author of *The Caine Mutiny* . . . Mr. Keefer" . . . and then dashes the drink into Keefer's face.

The picture was shot in and around Hawaii, Pearl Harbor Naval Station, San Francisco, Yosemite National Park, and at the Columbia Studios in Hollywood. The movie took 51 days to complete. Despite the misgivings of a few high-ranking officers, the Navy was generous in its cooperation. Two destroyer-minesweepers, one in San Francisco and one in Hawaii, were made available to the movie company. They were the USS *Thompson* (DMS-38) and the USS *Doyle* (DMS-34). The Navy also provided attack boats, marines, and an aircraft carrier. The Navy, however, did not want to be mentioned in

3. Cinema Texas Program Notes, *The Caine Mutiny*, Vol. 14, No. 2, March 1978, p. 2.

4. Columbia Pictures, *A Diamond Jubilee Celebration*, November 2, 1984, p. 2.

the film's credits, a customary thing to do. Kramer paid tribute to the Navy in another way. The movie's last frame stated "the dedication of this film is simple: To the United States Navy."

One of Kramer's major concerns was to make the typhoon scene real. It was an extremely important scene because it hinged on the pivotal question of the mutiny. Would the ship have gone down had Maryk not relieved Queeg? The typhoon was carefully staged in several of Columbia Studios sound stages. A tank carrying 700 gallons of water was set up to splash water down on replicas of the *Caine*'s super structures and wheelhouse. The occupants of the wheelhouse were to be thoroughly drenched. Hydraulic rockers were set in motion to simulate the pitching and rolling of a ship trying to stay afloat. Lightning was also simulated. The bluish-orange flashes that lit the deck were very effective in exposing the fear-frozen face of Captain Queeg.[5] Also used at the studio

were three different miniatures of the *Caine* and a full-sized half of the vessel. The United States Department of the Interior allowed the film company to use Yosemite National Park in the film's romantic sequences featuring Ensign Keith and May Wynn (May Wynn).

MR. ROBERTS

Like *The Caine Mutiny*, Warner Bros.' *Mr. Roberts* was a smash hit. Warner Bros. asked for full Navy cooperation, but were turned down because the Navy believed the captain's character that would be played by James Cagney was detrimental to the Navy's image. Director John Ford who himself had a distinguished career in the Navy during World War II and was now a Rear Admiral in the reserves would not accept this. He went directly to the Chief of Naval Operations (CNO) and the Navy

5. *New York Times*, August 23, 1953.

Captain James Cagney stands on his cargo ship looking at the famous palm tree deck in Warner's *Mr. Roberts*.

Mr. Roberts (Henry Fonda) and Doc (William Powell) are amazed by Ensign Pulver's (Jack Lemmon) obsession with women.

immediately relented. The production company was permitted to use the 172-foot cargo ship USS *Hewell* (AG-145) and was allowed to film at Midway Island and Hawaii (Kanehoe Bay). Admiral John Dale Price (Ret.) the former Vice-Chief of Naval Operations was made Technical Advisor. Ford directed some of the film's exterior sequences from a 120-year-old outrigger canoe formerly belonging to King Kamehemeha III of Hawaii. Studio craftsman built the famous captain's palm tree deck on the *Hewell* because ships of that class did not have one. It was torn down when the cargo ship resumed normal operations.

Henry Fonda, who played *Mr. Roberts* in 1,600 performances on the stage and director John Ford and his son-in-law Frank Nugent, a screenwriter, clashed over script and style changes. Ford wanted to make the film more slapstick and physical than the play. Fonda wor-

ried that these changes would take the subtlety out of the production. He and producer Leland Hayward felt the film version should use what had worked in the play. Fonda did not like Ford's rough-house humor and some enmity between the two men must have existed because Ford actually hit Fonda when he came over to visit one night. Ford, a heavy drinker, started drinking during the production and had to quit to undergo a gall bladder operation. Mervyn LeRoy succeeded Ford and tried to make it like the play. Later, Ford, said he did most of the picture while LeRoy argued that he shot 90% of the product. A final accounting of who directed what or how much will probably never occur.[6]

Mr. Roberts was completed in April 1955 and opened in Los Angeles in July of that year. Jack Lemmon received the 1955 Academy Award for Best Supporting Actor. It was

6. Toronto Film Society, *Film Buff Series, 1986-1987*, pp. 3-4.

also nominated as Best Picture and Sound Recording.

Mr. Roberts (Henry Fonda) is essentially the story about life on a small supply ship in the backwaters of the Pacific War. Though Lt. Roberts is an efficient cargo master on the ship, he wants to see action badly. Mr. Roberts sees a fast task force moving to battle and becomes even more resentful of his captain (James Cagney) who will not let him transfer. He is just too valuable to the captain who received a palm tree for excellence in cargo handling due in large part to Mr. Roberts' efficiency. The captain loves his palm tree; the crew sees it as a symbol of the captain's oppression. The ship's other officers have a growing contempt for this martinet. Doc (William Powell), the ship's doctor, does a splendid job of dealing with the psycho-somatic pains of a restive crew. Ensign Pulver (Jack Lemmon) is so innocuous that the captain is not even aware of his presence on the ship for 14 months. Pulver is a lazy guy who only thinks about women. The captain has disdain for all his officers; to him they are a bunch of smart-aleck college boys. Roberts insists on two things: a transfer to combat duty for himself and a well-earned liberty for the crew. Roberts tells the captain he will stop requesting a transfer if he agrees to give the crew liberty. The crew is given liberty and they tear the local town down. But when Roberts hears that the war in Europe is over and that time is running out for him to get in the fight, he loses his composure and throws the captain's palms tree overboard. The captain panics and calls for general quarters. Roberts is ordered to report to him. The crew is moved when they hear over the inter-com that Roberts had sacrificed his desire for a transfer for their chance at a liberty. The crew has a contest to see who can best forge the captain's signature on a transfer request. The transfer goes through and Roberts is assigned to a destroyer. The final scene takes place on the cargo ship a few weeks later when two letters arrive. In the first letter, Roberts tells Pulver to stick up for the crew. He also tells them all that he is grateful for their showing him that courage in the face of boredom is every bit as important as it is under fire. In the second letter, the crew learns that Mr. Roberts has been killed in action in a Kamikaze attack. In a fit of emotion, Pulver throws the captain's palm tree into the water. The captain now understands that the spirit of Mr. Roberts lives on.

Mr. Roberts wins the affection of the crew and is awarded their own medal, "The Order of the Palm Tree."

After hearing about Mr. Roberts' death, a defiant Ensign Pulver (Jack Lemmon) throws the captain's new palm tree into the ocean and storms into his office saying, "Now, what's this crud about no movies tonight?"

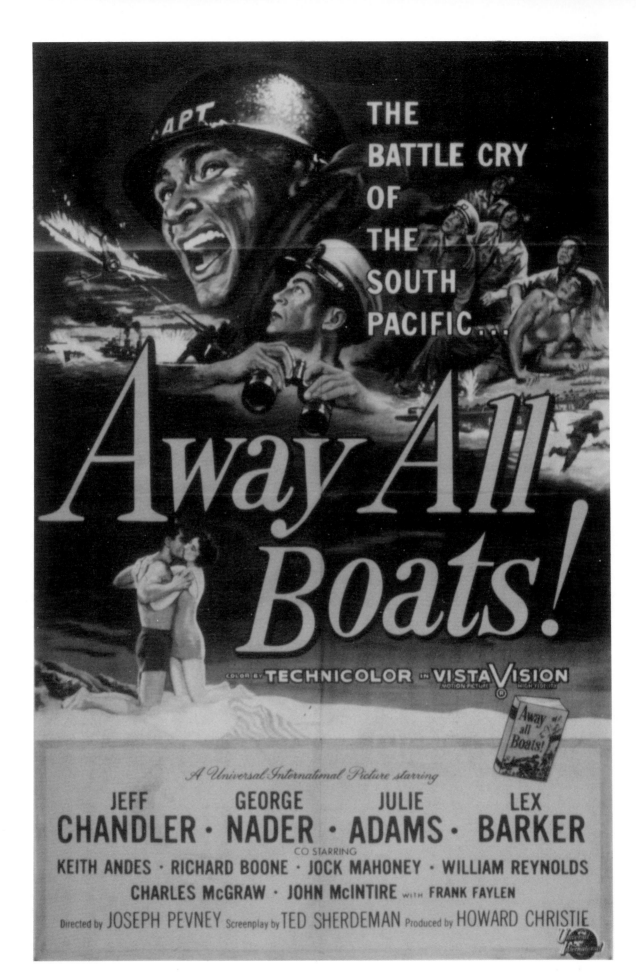

THE WAR STILL RAGES

Epic Battles, Biographies and Miscellany, 1956-1970

The remainder of the Hollywood films about the Navy in World World II made between 1956 and 1970 fall into four categories. The first grouping are films about actual historical events in the naval war in the Pacific. They are *Away All Boats* (1956), the story of naval amphibious operations in the Pacific from Makin Island to Okinawa; *In Harm's Way* (1965), which depicts naval activity from the Pearl Harbor attack to the Battle of the Philippines Sea; and *Tora! Tora! Tora!* (1970), an account of the Pearl Harbor attack.

A second category are film biographies. Included are *The Wings of Eagles* (1957) a biography of Commander Frank W. Wead, *The Gallant Hours* (1960), an account of the war experiences of Admiral William F. Halsey, Jr. and *PT 109* (1963), the story of the wartime seasoning of John F. Kennedy. Another grouping is made up of miscellaneous films about the Navy in World War II. They are *The Enemy Below* (1957) which details an encounter between an American destroyer-escort and a German U-Boat, *The Deep Six* (1958) which discusses the conflict between war and religion and *The Americanization of Emily* (1964) which debunks heroism in World War II. Finally, there are two comedies about the Navy that made their appearance in 1964. They are *Ensign Pulver* and *McHale's Navy*.

AWAY ALL BOATS

Universal-International's *Away All Boats* released in 1956 was the costliest picture ever made by that studio up to that time. The Navy liked the script and gave the production company its whole-hearted support, hailing the movie as the "best picture of Navy life ever made." This may have been a pointed dig by the Navy at the professional faults and psychotic eccentricities of naval officers as seen in the *Caine Mutiny*.[1] To be sure, Captain Jebidiah S. Hawks (Jeff Chandler) is the antithesis of Queeg. Hawks as commander of a large attack transport does his best to ready his crew for action. He is dutifully attached to his men, yet separated from them for command purposes; he can charm them and he can scare them. He believes that standing aloof in a command position is necessary to maintain a rigid code of discipline on his ship. Captain Hawks is a morale builder. He allows a pet monkey aboard as a mascot and orders a sailing sloop built for "yachting" during free time. In the tradition of John Paul Jones, Hawks gives his last ounce of strength and devotion to bring his crippled ship to a safe anchorage after a Japanese Kamikaze attack. Mortally wounded, he dies, but not before he makes a final effort to stand and see that his ship has made port.

Away All Boats first previewed at the Academy Award Theater in Los Angeles on May 8, 1956, shows the efforts of America's amphibious forces as they moved from Makin Island to Okinawa on their way to Japan. The fictional attack transport which is really the USS *Randall* (APA 224) is about the same size as a "liberty" ship. She carries a battalion of marines and was in the thick of the fighting.

This is one of the most authentic films ever made about the Navy. The studio was allowed to use the *Randall* and film the largest practice amphibious landings in the post-war period. Over 200 Navy ships and 10,000 marines participated in these war games in the Virgin Islands. Landings on the island of Vieques were perfect for the movie because the island's terrain approximates the topography of Guadalcanal and Saipan in the Pacific. Wide-screen Vista Vision and technicolor allows the movie-goer to see the full sweep of the "enemy" coast and witness a panoramic view of what an island assault in World War II may have looked like. Captain Robert Theobold (USN) of the *Belinda* (*Randall*) purposely sailed in lazy circles giving the camera

---

1. *Cue*, June 18, 1956.

crews the opportunity to shoot sequences showing the lowering of the landing craft and the use of shipboard defense systems. He changed course at least 50 times one day in order to allow the film makers the best sunlight conditions.

While it is known that Captain Hawks was disappointed at not getting command of a cruiser, he nonetheless puts his heart and soul into commanding the *Belinda*. He trains his crew with stop-watch exactness. He is fortunate to have Lt. MacDougal (George Nader) on board. This former merchant marine skipper becomes Hawks' "shadow" executive officer when the real one, Commander Quigly, up from the reserves, proves inexperienced. The movie, however, points out that the Navy is a good place to learn and grow and Quigly does so well that he is given a command of his own. The only romance in the movie is shown in flashbacks of MacDougal and his wife (Julie Adams). They personify love and respect for each other.

The climactic sequences in the film are shown in the invasion of Okinawa and the heavy Kamikaze counterattacks. One Kamikaze slams into the *Belinda*'s port side and another hits the bridge. Hawks is severely wounded and MacDougal takes command. With the ship foundering, MacDougal orders a compressor brought from the ship's fantail in order to force the water out through a tear in the ship's side; but when the propeller shaft snaps, he orders his landing craft to take the "mother" ship in tow. Safely at anchor, he sees the captain's final effort to look out of a port hole to see that the ship is safe.

The cinematic history of *Away All Boats* is unique in the annals of cooperation between commercial film companies and the Navy. When Edward Muhl, the studio's production manager asked the Navy whether the studio could coordinate their shooting schedule with future Navy amphibious landing maneuvers in the Caribbean, the answer was yes. Eight months before the exercise was to begin, the studio sent a group of executives to Vieques Island to scout the locale. It seemed perfect and the film company began making arrangements to send a technical crew of 120 to set up a location site some 5,000 miles away from Hollywood. The film company stayed in the area for six weeks. They stayed in several of the swank hotels in St. Thomas.

Cinematographer William Daniels had a field day filming the mock invasion of the island of the Vieques. Daniels used four Vistavision cameras each manned by a crew of four. One of the cameras was placed on Vieques beach-head, camouflaged behind a palm tree; another was mounted on the deck of the destroyer which darted through the invasion waters simulating gun cover for the assault. A third was placed on the bridge of the *Randall* and

a fourth was used on a helicopter hovering over the battle area.

The movie's interior shots were made in Hollywood. For this phase of the production, studio craftsman built a 111-foot replica of the *Belinda*'s (*Randall*) midsection. Under it, they placed hydraulic rams which by proper manipulation could almost instantaneously roll the midsection, rock it, plunge it, or even toss it anywhere within the angle of 45 degrees. This allowed director Joseph Pevney the means to duplicate any possible condition that might exist at sea.[2]

IN HARM'S WAY

In Harm's Way also tries to deal with the events of the Pacific War, but it is so mired down by the personal problems of its characters that the naval actions which it portrays comes out jumbled. Premiered at the Paramount Theater in Hollywood on April 6, 1965, the affair was staged with the cooperation of the Navy League's Youth Program. Attending were the usual mix of stars, politicians, and Navy brass. In one of the largest mass screenings of any movie, Producer Otto Preminger invited 10,000 military personnel and their wives for free showings at many of the Hawaiian military installations. Though Preminger worked with the full cooperation of the Defense Department, both the script and the technical aspects of the movie keep it from being a good picture. As basically a melodrama which focuses on the lives of people and fighting a war in its first year, it both fails as a presentation of real people and an authentic recreation of the Pearl Harbor attack and naval operations thereafter. During the almost three hours of this sensationalized view of World War II, the movie shows rape, suicide, assorted romances and 1940-style heroics. The Navy in this movie seems to only serve as a back-drop for a soap-opera like story.

The depiction of the Pearl Harbor attack itself is a case in point. Instead of using stock footage about the attack that was available and showing the destruction of the fleet, Preminger is satisfied to move the cruiser USS *St. Paul* (CA-73) and the destroyer USS *Phillip* (DD-498) around the harbor aimlessly with the destroyer dashing through the channel out to sea. It is known that no ship would risk being sunk in the channel thereby bottling up the entire fleet.

The last battle sequence which shows a Japanese fleet centered around the battleship *Yamato* bearing down on

2. Universal International Production Story, *Away All Boats*, pp. 6-12. Academy of Motion Picture Arts and Sciences, Margaret Herrick Library, Beverly Hills, CA.

In the film *In Harm's Way* Henry Fonda is again cast as Admiral Chester Nimitz.

A graying Dana Andrews plans for future action with his subordinates.

an American beachhead does not look real. The Japanese ship miniatures which were as large as 55 feet in length look no better than radio-controlled commercial models. The highly toted battle sounds hailed by the studio as being fully researched do not make the battle scene any more genuine. Yet technicians were able to acquire C-47s and a loaned B-25 after the government informed them that they had none. Captain Eddington (Kirk Douglas), the perverse rapist, is killed in the PB-J (Navy version of a B-25) later as he finds the Japanese fleet approaching an island landing and dies in a blaze of glory.

The well-organized production company with its headquarters in the brand-new *Ilikai* Hotel in Waikiki used 22 different locations throughout Hawaii. Nonetheless, a *New York Times* review states: "Mr. Preminger is nothing if not generous. He gives you a lot of bang for the buck. He simply neglects to make it have the hard, crushing sound and the feel of truth."[3]

3. *New York Times*, April 7, 1965.

A real destroyer-escort underway lends credibility to *In Harm's Way*.

Though this miniature of a Japanese destroyer was costly, it still did not look real in *In Harm's Way* sequences.

TORA! TORA! TORA!

Tora! Tora! Tora! was the second most expensive picture (*Cleopatra* was the first) ever made up until that time. It cost $25,000,000 and took three years and eight months to make. The question is, why would Fox and the Defense Department want to make a movie about one of America's great defeats? In response to congressional critics, some of whom felt that the movie would glorify Japan and others who wanted to limit military cooperation between Hollywood film companies, Darryl Zanuck, president of Twentieth Century Fox placed a full-page ad in both the *New York Times* and the *New York Post*. In bold type he said that *Tora! Tora! Tora!* had been officially approved by both the American and Japanese Departments of Defense and that its purpose was to educate the American public about the need for preparedness in this "acute missile age where a sneak attack could occur at any moment." Furthermore, he said, the American people cannot be moved by simply showing movies where we always win. The American people, he continued, should be reminded that they are not invincible and have been successfully attacked.[4] Finally, he concluded that the film is a reminder of a tragic event that occurred before and must never happen again.

The only serious dispute that the studio had with the Navy was over using the USS *Yorktown* (CV-10) as a Japanese aircraft carrier in the movie. Japan had lost all her aircraft carriers in World War II. Luckily, the impropriety of using an American carrier as a Japanese man-of-war did not bother any groups in the United States. Because aircraft operations were a risky business, safety factors alone may have ended the project before it got started. A great worry was the possibility of an air crash on the carrier either during take-offs or landings. Under-Secretary of Defense Paul Nitze worked-out a compromise plan. The "Pearl Harbor raiders" would be able to take off, but not land on the carrier. Nitze was willing to take this gamble because he wanted the film made. Like Zanuck, he saw the picture as a part of American history and that it was valuable that American audiences should know that in war "you have victory and you have defeat." The Navy's Media Relations Division was relieved by this decision because a refusal of this kind might set a precedent detrimental to some of their forth-coming projects, like the movie *Midway.*[5]

Tora! Tora! Tora! is the best and the technically most accurate dramatization of the Japanese attack on Pearl Harbor ever made. As film reviewer Charles Champlin writes: "Pearl Harbor on December 7, 1941, cannot have looked or sounded or felt greatly different than this."[6] The films consists of two segments, one American and the other Japanese with cross-cutting and integration between them. The movie does not discuss the issue of causation in any detail and glosses over the geo-political clashes the two powers had. Few value judgments are made. Hollywood screenwriter Larry Forrester spent 18 months writing the script using about 70 books to make the Pearl Harbor attack both factual and clear. The film is divided into two parts, the Japanese decision and planning for the attack and the attack itself. The viewer sees that the Japanese army wants war against the Americans in order to have a freer hand in Asia. The Navy's mission is to destroy the only force capable of containing that expansion. It is the United States Fleet at Pearl Harbor. Admiral Yamamoto, lukewarm about any sustained fight with the Americans, organizes the attack brilliantly. He, nonetheless, worries that even a successful attack might only result in the awakening of a "sleeping (American) giant." On the other hand, the Americans are seen as being aware that an attack is coming, but not sure where. Some think it will be the Philippines. American military intelligence breaks the Japanese code, but is not organized to take advan-

4. *The Hollywood Reporter*, June 17, 1969.

5. Lawrence Suid, *Guts in Glory: Great American War Movies* (Addison-Wesley Publishing Co., 1976), p. 281.

6. *Los Angeles Times*, September 23, 1970.

Airmen scramble as Japanese Zeros attack plywood replicas of P-40 aircraft at Wheeler Field in *Tora! Tora! Tora!*

tage of it. The best example of this is when a commercial telegram is tardily sent to both Army and Navy commanders that an attack is imminent. While the Japanese seem flawless in their "sneak" attack, the Americans are ill-prepared. Admiral Kimmel and General Short do not receive the latest intelligence reports until it is too late. The Japanese seem to be at their best when the attack comes; the Americans are shocked and surprised. Even last minute chances to prepare for the onslaught come to naught. The Navy fails to report the sightings of a Japanese mini-sub trying to enter Pearl Harbor. The efficient use of radar on the northwest part of Oahu could have given the Americans more time to get ready.

The Department of Defense was very generous to Twentieth Century Fox in the making of the film. It allowed them to shoot sequences at many of the sites that were attacked on December 7, 1941, including Ford Island and "battleship row," where much of the battleline of the U.S. Navy was destroyed, Wheeler Field, Schofield Barracks, and Fort Schafter.

The biggest problem in a production of this magnitude was acquiring ships to depict the actual events. Fox's miniature department was put to work and built 19 Japanese and 10 American warships. The ships averaged 40 feet in length and were built either to the scale of ½ inch to the foot or ¾ inch to the foot depending on whether they would be blown up in the movie or not. The larger the scale of the miniature, the more realistic the explosion would look. Exacting replicas of key ships for important sequences were built in Hawaii and Japan. The Dillingham Corporation of Honolulu built a full-size section of the USS *Arizona* (BB-39) which was mounted on two steel barges and towed to "battleship row." Her guns of .30 calibre to five inch actually functioned. This section also doubled as the *Nevada* (BB-36), the *Oklahoma* (BB-37), and the *West Virginia* (BB-48). Dillingham also constructed a mast of the *Tennessee* (BB-43) with its distinctive gun control tower. Aligned with the background of the doomed *Arizona* as it was, the tragedy of the battle fleet could be stated perfectly. In addition to these mock-ups, the Navy loaned the studio six warships. Included were four destroyer types, a minesweeper, and the aircraft carrier USS *Yorktown* (CV-10). The *Yorktown* was indispensable as she doubled for the attacking Japanese carrier *Akagi*. A full-scale replica of Admiral Yamamoto's flagship the battleship *Nagato* was constructed in Japan. It was on this ship's foredeck that the admiral watched his torpedo planes practice in the summer of 1941. Also built in Japan were three-quarters of the carrier *Akagi*, Admiral Nagumo's flagship in the Pearl Harbor attack.[7]

As no Japanese aircraft were available for the film, Fox created its own air force by modifying existing American World War II training planes. They would play the role of the 353 planes which took part in the attack. Actually, only some 30 planes were refashioned. American AT-6s and BT-13s were modified to look like three types of Japanese aircraft of Nagumo's strike force. This group consisted of twelve Mitsubishi A6M2 "Zeros" (AT-6s), nine Aichi Type "Vals" (BT-13s), and nine "Kates" (an AT-6/BT-13 combination). In addition, another 21 AT-6s were turned over to the Japanese who used them in carrier sequences filmed at Ahiya AFB, Japan. It took about three months and $8,000,000 to restage the air attacks. 35 hours of combat footage was shot. The bombing and strafing of American P-40 fighter plane replicas at Wheeler Field was visually one of the more spectacular scenes in the film.[8]

Yet there are a number of reasons why this striking movie, now a film classic, did not make money at the box office. First of all 1970, the year of its release, was a time of heightened anti-Vietnam War fury in the United States. Second, some reviewers were not pleased that the film did not develop its characters to a greater extent and felt that the movie failed to generate the needed drama. Apparently not enough of the American people wanted to see a movie about a pivotal event in their history with its "wake-up" call for an adequate defense in the missile age. Thus, the inattention given here to the so-called power of the "Military-Celluloid Complex" may have been one of the reasons why Hollywood ended the cycle of service movies which had begun twenty years earlier.

During the post-war cycle of films, movies were made about two of the most dramatic military leaders in the Second World War. The Academy Award winning *Patton* (1970) and *MacArthur* (1977) were both successful movie biographies. Although the Navy had a large pool of admirals with cunning and skill, only Admiral William F. "Bull" Halsey had a movie biography made about him and that was limited to the Guadalcanal campaign. The other biographies made about men in the naval service during the Second World War were *PT 109* (1963),

the wartime experiences of John F. Kennedy and *The Wings of Eagles* (1957), the life and times of naval officer and screenwriter Commander Frank. W. Wead.

7. Final Information Guide for *Tora! Tora! Tora!*, p. 4-12. Academy of Motion Picture Arts and Sciences. Margaret Herrick Library, Beverly Hills, CA.

8. Bruce W. Orriss, *When Hollywood Ruled the Skies* (Hawthorne: Aero Associates, 1948), pp. 196-98.

The battleship *Nagato*, 660 feet in length, was reconstructed of wood from the original plans. It was the largest film set ever built in Japan and was used for filming for seven weeks. Another set was constructed of the *Akagi*'s hangar deck. Both sets were constructed at Ashuyu on the island of Kyushu. OTTO LANG PHOTOS

THE WINGS OF EAGLES

Frank W. Wead's writings and credits appeared on more movies about the Navy than any other man in the 1930s and 1940s.[9] While it is impossible to measure a writer's impact on his audience, there is no doubt that Wead's pen influenced the public greatly with his books, magazine articles, and motion pictures. Wead's vision of the Navy, its traditions, esprit d'corps, code of honor, and commitment to efficiency are ever present in his works. Among his successful original stories and screenplays were *Helldivers* (1932), *Submarine D-1* (1937), *Sailor's Lady* (1940), *Dive Bomber* (1941), *Destroyer* (1943), and *They Were Expendable* (1945).

Frank (Spig) Wead, the subject of the movie, had an interesting if somewhat troubled life. Born in 1895 in Peoria, Illinois, the son of an attorney, Wead's childhood ambition was to become a naval officer. He graduated from the Naval Academy in 1916 with honors. In the Great War, he participated in the North Sea mine barrage. After the war, he became interested in aviation and received his wings at Pensacola. As a Navy flyer, he commanded the American squadron that won the coveted Snyder Cup in 1923. The holder of five world records in naval aviation, Wead became an early advocate of carrier aviation and commanded the first squadron of planes to operate from a carrier.

As a result of an accident in his home in 1926, Wead became a paraplegic; his naval career was abruptly ended. He recovered slowly with the help of friends who stuck by him. He became a writer and slowly acquired writing techniques alone. First, he learned story construction and then added suspense and emotion according to his feeling about the characters involved. He wrote for aviation trade journals at the beginning and then began writing fiction for pulp magazines. He then went on to write for the so-called "slick" magazines including the *Saturday Evening Post*. Wead's first successful play was *Ceiling Zero*. From his success on Broadway, he went to Hollywood where he worked with John Ford, Warner Bros. and other studios. He was especially successful in writing screenplays and stories about the Navy.[10]

Despite his tremendous physical handicap, Wead returned to the Navy during World War II. He first worked in the office of the air-minded Admiral John Towers and later was sent to Rhode Island to assemble new carrier air groups. It was at this time that he conceived the idea that large attack carriers needed the backing of "jeep" or "baby" carriers which could replace aircraft and air crews quickly when the larger carriers needed them. Wead saw combat aboard a large carrier in the Marshall Islands. After suffering a heart attack, he returned to Hollywood where he wrote the screenplay for *They Were Expendable*. Wead died at the age of 52 in 1947. The motion picture *The Wings of Eagles* went into production almost a decade later and was considered a memorial to "Spig" Wead. His interesting career and unusual struggle to overcome his paralysis should have led to a respectful and dignified presentation of his life. Unfortunately, it did not.

Despite the fact that Director John Ford and Wead were good friends, Wead does not come off as a real person in the story. This may be because of the Fenton-Haines screenplay or even Ford's direction of John Wayne who played Wead. Ford did have mixed feelings about doing the movie. He supposedly told Peter Bagdonovich later he really did not want to make that movie, but did not want anyone else to make it either.[11]

Wead, himself, who was not overly sentimental, probably would not have liked many of the things shown in the movie. He may have seen fact and fiction in a mix. The stunt flying sequence in Pensacola by a man just learning to fly is ridiculous; so were the Army and Navy fisticuffs and the cake throwing that was repeated. The many references to booze, especially in the hospital seem out of place. "Spig's" off and on again relationship with his wife Minnie (Maureen O'Hara) is not dealt with adequately, though there are hints his dedication to the Navy may have been a source of conflict or that even alcoholism was involved. Dan Daily's characterization of Wead's favorite Chief Petty Officer Carson seems contrived, though it allows for some humor. Ward Bond does a brilliant job of portraying Director Dodge, a character who is unmistakenly John Ford. He plays it splendidly, but the part's short duration shows that Wead's Hollywood years are skimmed over. We see no more than a meager clip from Ford and Wead's *Hell Divers* (1932), where Clark Gable and Wallace Beery were in a drunken brawl in Panama. Wead's life in Hollywood simply does not get the attention it deserves. This production which is aimed at a masculine audience, carries on with the traditional naval stereotypes, like the gruff admiral, the homely nurse, and the dumb gunner's mate.

Film locations of this picture were San Diego Naval Hospital, Pensacola Naval Air Station, and the aircraft carrier USS *Philippine Seas* (CV-48) off the coast of California. The sentimentality attached to the scene where Wead is being removed from a ship on a bosun's chair after his heart attack is dramatic, even though the real Wead might not have liked it.

9. *Los Angeles Times*, February 10, 1957.

10. *MGM Biographical Information on Frank W. Wead, January 2, 1944* and *Columbia Studios Biography* in Biography File of Frank W. Wead, Academy of Motion Picture Arts and Sciences, Margaret Herrick Library, Beverly Hills, CA.

11. *Cinema Texas Program Notes*, Vol. 19, November 19, 1980, p. 29.

John Wayne and an Army flyer shove cake at each other in an Army-Navy brawl in MGM's *Wings of Eagles*.

After a tragic accident, Frank Wead (John Wayne) slowly regains hope with the help of devoted friends played by Ken Curtis, Dan Dailey, and Tige Andrews.

THE GALLANT HOURS

Another biography about a prominent naval personality was brought to the screen in 1960. *The Gallant Hours* starring James Cagney and directed by Robert Montgomery was about Admiral William F. Halsey Jr. It traced his life as the commander of American naval forces in the Guadalcanal campaign from October 18 to November 15, 1942. This was not Cagney's first picture about the Navy. In 1934, he played an ordinary sailor stationed on the USS *Arizona* in *Here Comes the Navy*. His distinctive style helped make it a popular movie and it was brought back to the screen in late 1940 as World War II heated up.[12] If the public liked him, the officers on the Navy's Motion Picture Board would have preferred someone else to represent their image on the screen. When Frank Wead told a number of them that Cagney was not slated to play in the 1937 movie *Submarine D-1* some of them cheered. The dislike of Cagney may have been due to their taboo against allowing actors with "bad" guy images to play naval officers. In a letter to a Warner Bros. executive, Wead wrote that while the Navy people hate his guts (Cagney), it's not his fault, adding that: "they shouldn't take actors seriously."[13] Despite all this rancor, Cagney did play in *Devil Dogs of the Air* (1935), *The Fighting 69th* (1940), and *Captains of the Clouds* (1942). His next important Navy role was the captain of the little cargo ship the USS *Hewell* in *Mr. Roberts* in 1955. Many career officers may have been tickled when they heard the captain (James Cagney), fearful that Mr. Roberts' transfer might hurt his career exclaim: "I got a reputa-

tion with the admiral and I ain't gonna lose it on account of any letter written by some smart-aleck college officer."[14] By 1960 Cagney was ready and available to play the part of Admiral Halsey in *The Gallant Hours*. This movie was successful for two important reasons. Both Cagney and Robert Montgomery admired Halsey greatly and Cagney bore a great resemblance to the fighting admiral.

The Gallant Hours which premiered at the Keith Theater in Washington D.C. on May·13, 1960, focuses on the personal side of Admiral Halsey's experiences during the bloody Guadalcanal Campaign. There are no naval battles in this motion picture. The movie portrays a kinder Halsey and suggests that his opprobrium against the Japanese enemy such as "the only good Jap is a dead one" are not heartfelt and are really for the press and his men's morale. Halsey is seen as a man who agonizes during the battles and tells those around him that he will "never forget the boys who died."

A very important feature in the film is his duel with Japanese Admiral Yamamoto (James Gotto). Both men are characterized as superb and daring commanders. Each plays hunches and makes decisions with courageous finality. Because he has a premonition, Yamamoto watches for Halsey's arrival on Guadalcanal in order to shoot his plane down. Halsey somehow lands elsewhere safely. When Yamamoto sends his fleet to engage Halsey's out-

12. "Warner's Exploit Sheet," Production Papers, *Here Comes the Navy*, Warner Bros. Archives, U.S.C.

13. Letter from Frank Wead to Lou Edelman, November 24, 1936, *Submarine D-1*, Production Papers, Warner Bros. Archives, U.S.C.

14. *Mr. Roberts Final Script*, p. 52, Warner Bros. Archives, U.S.C.

Admiral William "Bull" Halsey (James Cagney) flying into the Solomens plays a hunch and changes his course, which saved his life by avoiding a Japanese shoot-down in United Artist's *The Gallant Hours*.

numbered forces, the American gives his noted order: "attack-repeat-attack." Despite heavy losses including the sinking of the USS *Hornet* (CV-8), the Americans drive the enemy forces back to their base at Truk. These are indeed the *Gallant Hours* when the United States alters the direction of the Pacific War. One episode, however, goes a little too far in its "literary license" when the movie tries to round off its duel of the admirals. Though Halsey knew Yamamoto's inspection timetable and ordered the destruction of the Japanese Fleet Admiral's plane, this did not occur during the time frame of this picture. That event did not happen until the spring of 1943.[15]

James Cagney was perfect for the part of Halsey. The two bore a great resemblance to each other. Cagney said the only make-up he used was a coat of tan. He also combed up his eyebrows to approximate the admiral's own bushy ones. Cagney also studied Halsey's mannerism of which there were almost none; he had to make sure that his own unique style did not intrude in his characterization of the admiral. Director Robert Montgomery, who had served with the admiral in the Solomons, took special care to minimize Cagney's distinctive mannerism.

Thus in his portrayal of naval personalities, James Cagney starts out as an argumentative gob in *Here Comes the Navy*, moves on to play a grouchy, lazy almost idiotic captain of a cargo ship in *Mr. Roberts*. From there, he finishes his "naval" career playing a deeply motivated and brilliant admiral in *The Gallant Hours*.

PT 109

The last biographical picture made during this period was the controversial movie *PT 109*. Produced by Warner Bros. under the supervision of Jack L. Warner himself, the film was released in 1963 about six months before the Kennedy assassination. A movie about the heroics of an incumbent president who was planning to run for a second term was unheard of up until this time. Because of the political stakes involved, every attempt to keep the film from becoming controversial was made. Kennedy had liked Robert J. Donovan's book *PT109* and he and his advisors approved the Warner Bros. script as well. Shrewd politicians are, however, not scenarioists and so they lack the experience to anticipate some of the drawbacks the film might have. Initially, Kennedy wanted Warren Beatty to play the lead, but settled for the young Cliff Robertson. With everyone's eyes riveted on the president and wary of any negative political consequences, all agreed that the film should be made carefully. Producer Bryan Foy went so far as to check into whether anyone in the cast might have a communist

President Kennedy initially wanted Warren Beatty to play the lead role in *PT 109*, but agreed to Cliff Robertson.

background or any other embarrassing problem. The question of naval cooperation, always a sensitive issue, was handled with careful restraint. Technical Advisor for the film, Captain Jack E. Gibson, was asked to send a weekly written report to CHINFO (Naval Chief of Information). The Navy did provide a destroyer and six other ships in the filming, but rejected Warner's request for using Navy planes in the picture's several air sequences. When the Navy could not provide the studio with the PT-Boats needed in the film because none were in service, Warner Bros. obtained boat plans from General Dynamics and purchased three air-sea rescue boats they planned to convert.[16]

Succumbing to all kinds of outside pressures, screen writer Richard L. Breen put forth a script which portrayed JFK as an almost perfect man with an upbeat personality. The story tends, however, to undercut the real factual heroism of Lt. (J.G.) Kennedy when he is made into a super-hero. Moreover, the script seems to exaggerate the actions of the PT-Boats in the Solomons. Bryan Foy, who saw the picture's box-office potential, liked the script

15. Samuel Elliot Morison, *The Two Ocean War* (Boston: Little Brown and Company, 1963), p. 274.

16. Memo, March 2, 1962, *PT 109*, Production Papers, Warner Bros. Archives, U.S.C.

Kennedy swims for his life when his boat is rammed by a Japanese destroyer.

Kennedy scrawls a message on a coconut that will later bring a rescue party.

PT 157 arrives from Rendova and rescues Kennedy and his crew.

and did not want to change it. On the other hand, veteran director Lewis Milestone felt some strategic changes had to be made in it. He especially did not like the profusion of comedic lines in the story. He called them "cornball" and insisted on a greater artistic dimension. The feud ended when Jack L. Warner sided with Foy and Milestone was fired.[17]

The premiere of *PT 109* was held on July 2, 1963, at the Beverly Hilton Hotel where $133,000 was raised for the Joseph P. Kennedy Jr. Foundation for retarded youngsters. The motif of the gala event was patriotic with red, white, and blue floral pieces at each table. The dessert was formed into a replica of *PT 109*. It was carried on the shoulders of several waiters. The Kennedy family was there in strength. A message was expected from President Kennedy, but it never arrived.

In the story JFK is seen as a likeable, happy-go-lucky junior officer who volunteers for PT-Boat service. He takes over *PT 109* and bonds with a fighting crew who are good-natured, comedic and abnormally, perhaps, unrealistically handsome. His executive officer on the 109 is Lt. Leonard Thom (Ty Harden) who smiles a great deal of the time. At first, Kennedy gets little support from the group's maintenance officer Comdr. Ritchie (James Gregory), but we see later that this First World War vet isn't a bad guy at all. JFK's first assignment is to get to Choissel Island and pick up some marines who are under attack. He succeeds in his task, but runs out of fuel. Under Japanese fire, the boat is towed back to the base.

On August 2, 1943, when on patrol, a Japanese destroyer cuts *PT 109* in two and destroys her. JFK swims 3½ miles to Plum Pudding Island. In an act of courage and compassion, he breast strokes to safety with

a badly burned crew member and saves his life. At night, JFK treads water and waits for a patrol in Ferguson Channel, but none arrives. Kennedy moves to another island where he scratches out a message on a coconut and gives it to friendly natives. He writes that eleven men are alive and that they need a small boat to get back to Rendova. They make it back to the base. He declines a transfer home at this point and declares "I'd like to stay for a few more innings." He takes over another boat, the PT-59 and continues the war. He is good-natured and even-tempered.

Most of the action sequences were filmed at Big Pine Key (Munson Island, Florida). The island, just 25 miles from Key West is gnat-ridden and mosquito infested. It is similar to Tulagi, Solomon Islands in the July heat. Warner Bros. poured 15 gallons of pesticide daily on the island. Four members of the film company were bitten by scorpions, but the cast was delighted it could stay in Key West nightly. There at the Holiday Inn, they groused about the 134 page script which some felt was as dull as Munson Island. As they settled into their tasks, most of them began to see the picture as not about a president, but a typical young naval officer doing his job in the South Pacific.[18]

As a result of the Kennedy assassination which occurred on November 22, 1963, all prints of *PT 109* were withdrawn. Warner Bros. productions felt it would be in bad taste to show the film during a national period of mourning. The motion picture had been released six months before the assassination and would have taken normally eighteen months to complete its normal cycle through 15,000 theaters.[19]

17. "Feud Rocks PT 109," undated and unsourced, Production Papers, *PT 109*, Academy of Motion Picture Arts and Sciences, Margaret Herrick Library, Beverly Hills, CA.

18. Production Papers, *PT 109*, Warner Bros. Archives, U.S.C.

19. *Los Angeles Times*, Dec. 5, 1963.

THE ENEMY BELOW

Although considered one of the top motion pictures of 1957 by the National Board of Reviews and *Time* magazine, Twentieth Century Fox's *The Enemy Below* did not fare well at the box office. Latent anti-war feelings and the absence of women in this drama may have made the film unappealing to a large part of the viewing public. The Defense Department and the Navy approved of the movie and cooperated with Fox to the fullest extent. Recruitment and maintaining a positive image was their motive. The inclusion of a sub-plot which differentiated "good" Germans from the Nazi's paralleled United States foreign policy as it sought to build up West German power in NATO. Hence, Commander Von Stolberg (Curt Jurgens), the U-Boat commander, is characterized as a three-dimensional person, a notion that would never have been allowed on the screen during the war. He is a cunning anti-Nazi warrior who much prefers World War I over Hitler's War. Von Stolberg believes honor and God are lacking in the "new" Germany. He grieves that science with its radar and sonar have taken precedence over the skill and the determination of the warrior. Yet duty keeps him in the German Navy. The American destroyer commander Murrell (Robert Mitchum) is himself a calculating and experienced seaman who is every bit as skilled as his adversary. Unlike the book *The Enemy Below*, by Commander D.A. Raynor, R.N., this production fails to develop fully the relish with which both commanders conduct their cat-and-mouse game at sea.

The major theme in this story is the out-witting, out-guessing and out-waiting game played by the two enemies. Commander Murrell is a very competent seaman who needs to prove himself before his crew because he is from the merchant marine. He is quickly able to do that and is no longer seen as just a plain "feather merchant." He does not show any hatred or bitterness towards the Germans even though his wife was a victim of a U-Boat attack. He focuses on the job at hand. Both men use the technology available on their ships; both men use their intellect in this dangerous duel. After their paths have crossed, the American deduces that the U-Boat is holding a constant course because it is on a special mission. He guesses correctly, the submarine is trying to rendezvous with another German ship to deliver a secret code book. The U-Boat fires four torpedoes which miss the destroyer. In order to avoid the constant depth-charging that follows, the German drops to the ocean floor where a waiting game ensues. Von Stolberg shows his humane side when he comforts a berserk crewman. In a stroke of luck, the German positions himself to use his last torpedo. It hits the destroyer and Murrell quickly sets fires

on his main deck and orders his crew to abandon ship to try to exaggerate his predicament. Von Stolberg takes the bait and surfaces in order to finish off the Americans with his deck gun. The German is surprised when he is met by counter-fire. The climax of the confrontation is when the U.S. destroyer rams the U-Boat, destroying both ships. Before the film's final release, producer Dick Powell experimented with two different endings. The first one showed both commanders surviving and saluting one another as they were picked up by a third American ship. The other version shows both captains perishing with their ships. Before live audiences, Powell chose the happier of the two fade-outs.

Movie locations for this film were Hawaii and the coast of California off Long Beach. The USS *Whitehurst* (DE-634), a veteran of Kamikaze attacks during the Second World War was loaned to Fox. Its name was changed to the fictional USS *Haynes* (DE-181). For accuracy, the ship's numbers were changed to a smaller World War II configuration on her prow. For the same reason, potato-peeling by the crew was reintroduced to the ship. Much of the action was filmed inside Pearl Harbor near the sunken USS *Arizona*. Realistic abandon-ship procedures were taken in this sequence. The USS *Alfred E. Cunningham* (DD-752), picked up the survivors of both the *Haynes* and the U-boat in the film's final collision scene off Long Beach.[20] Only mock-ups were used for the submarine sequences. A serious accident occurred on the *Whitehurst* some 18 miles off Hawaii when eleven depth-charges prematurely exploded forty yards off the ship's stern. One of the ship's engines was knocked out. The press, however, incorrectly reported that the ship nearly sank and that the accident was due to Robert Mitchum's giving the wrong order.[21] Untrue, the incident was really caused by a communication gaffe. Nonetheless, a hi-fi system was later presented to the crew of the *Whitehurst* for their cooperation; a helpful Navy tug was also presented with a washing machine for its help in the production.

THE DEEP SIX

As in *The Enemy Below*, Warner Bros. Jaguar Production's *The Deep Six* is also about destroyer duty, but this time in the North Pacific. The film, in fact, is dedicated to the Navy's Destroyer Force. The officers and men of the USS *Stephen Potter* (DD-538) are acknowledged in

20. Vital Statistics on "The Enemy Below," Production Papers *The Enemy Below*, Academy of Motion Picture Arts and Sciences, Margaret Herrick Library, Beverly Hills, CA.

21. *Los Angeles Times*, June 7, 1957.

Curt Jurgens is not the typical German officer American movie-goers were accustomed to. Here we see him and Theodore Bickel encouraging the U-Boat crew during a desperate time in *The Enemy Below.*

In the final climax of the film, the American destroyer rams the U-Boat which was actually a clever mock-up.

the film's credits as well. Because Navy regulations require that the ship's name and numbers be changed in making movies, the *Potter*, veteran of the Pacific War and Korea, was renamed the USS *Poe* (DD-482), an unused name and number. For the sake of authenticity, all obvious changes or improvements on Navy destroyers since 1942, were removed. For example, Warner Bros. installed 20 mm guns for the filming of the movie. As interesting as it may have been for crew members watching the movie "takes" aboard ship, some of them were not happy about having to clean up the debris caused by movie-made "explosions" even if it was only harmless cork they had to sweep up. As the *Potter* (*Poe*), star of the Hollywood movie, steamed out of its base at Long Beach for a location site, a likely message from a passing Navy ship's signal lamp might read: "What movie stars have you got aboard today?"

It took producer Martin Rackin five months to get Navy approval for the film because of its controversial nature. The Navy finally accepted the script when it was changed to suit interests of the Defense Department and the Navy.[22]

The Deep Six which simply means in Navy jargon burial at sea is the story of a young reserve officer Lt. Austen (Alan Ladd) who is called up to active duty. Assigned to the destroyer *Poe*, the former artist becomes the ship's gunnery officer. Lt. Austen is not the ship's most adjusted officer because he brings to his job some deep-seated problems such as his Quaker pacifism instilled in him as a child. Furthermore, he still has peaceful artistic leanings. Though he thinks that his Quaker faith and its traditions are no longer factors in his life, his belief in non-violence is still a part of his world view. His anguish as to whether to fight or not become the central theme in the story. One wonders why he did not become a conscientious objector or transfer to a non-combatant branch of the service. Yet, here he is standing watch as a gunnery officer in the North Pacific. The first incident where his inner-conflict is tested is when he orders his gun crew to hold its fire on an intruding aircraft. As it turns out, the plane is identified as friendly and he is given undeserved credit for his alertness. However, he is demoted to damage control officer when he tells the captain (James Whitmore) the truth. The crew looks down on him and it is not until he removes an unexploded bomb on the ship that he wins back their respect. Slowly, his anger for the enemy begins to grow when he sees that it is not wrong to fight when you are in the right. He volunteers for a hazardous mission to rescue some Americans on a remote Aleutian island. But his latent pacifism reemerges when the Americans get into a fire-fight with enemy soldiers and he is hesitant

to fight back. It is only after his friend "Frenchy" Shapiro (William Bendix) is hit that Austen fires his weapon in anger. He now leaves behind his pacifist heritage. After being wounded, he is flown home where his girl (Dianne Foster) is waiting for his return. They will marry and he will return to his career as an artist.

The characters in *The Deep Six* may be more serious than those in *Mr. Roberts*, a film that it is compared to,

22. *New York Times*, July 7, 1957.

Lt. Austen (Alan Ladd) regains the respect of his shipmates when he removes an unexploded bomb from the deck of his destroyer in *The Deep Six.*

but they are not necessarily more realistic. The straight-out type of man that Mr. Roberts is is far more exciting than Austen whose character suggests that Quakers are not very firm in their convictions. Comdr. Meredith (James Whitmore) the *Poe*'s captain, is seen as a strong traditional officer who is flexible enough to give Austen another chance. "Frenchy" Shapiro is a good-natured chief who left his delicatessen and family to join the Navy. He is sympathetic to Austen's dilemma. The *Poe*'s executive officer is Lt. Cmdr. Edge (Keenan Wynn). Obsessed with the hatred of the Japanese enemy because of a friend's death on the *Arizona* on December 7, 1941, the severely ill officer is caught stealing morphine from the infirmary to lessen his pain. The ship's doctor, Lt. Blanchard (Efrem Zimbalist, Jr.) shows some understanding of Edge. Finally, Ski Krakowski (Joey Bishop) plays the role of the stereotypical gob who has a girl in every port, including "Kayak Kattie" in the Aleutian Islands.

THE AMERICANIZATION OF EMILY

By the 1960s, some war movies began to portray the military in a negative light. Wary of the heavy burden of defense expenditures and the prospect of nuclear war, some writers, journalists, and movie-makers turned to pacifist themes. One such movie which satirizes and ridicules the Navy in World War II is MGM's *The Americanization of Emily*, released in late 1964. Ideas expounded in this movie are relevant to all of the services because

it was basically an anti-war film. The main theme of the film expressed by Lt. Cmdr. Charles E. Madison (James Garner) is that war would disappear if the glory, nobility, and virtue were taken out of it. A corollary to this negation of warlike symbols is a new kind of "cowardice." Madison believes that if soldiers would run after the first shot was fired, there would not be a second shot. He ignores the fact that cowardice could lead to the take-over of the world by warped personalities like Hitler and Stalin or that cowards have historically made the best slaves. In preaching this gospel of cowardice, the movie suggests that the poor "grunts" who get killed in a war are neither brave nor noble, but gullible fools. While other movies have debunked war before, generally none of them have belittled the little guy who gets killed. Others might say that while he may have been a victim of injustice, he had at least tried to preserve his own dignity and did not run away.[23] The picture became a cult film during the Viet Nam era in the late '60s and early '70s. It helped support the prevalent notion in some quarters that it was better to be a live coward than a dead hero. The phrase "what if they gave a war and nobody came" is another expression of the same thing.

The Americanization of Emily opened at the Stanley Warner Theater in Beverly Hills on December 25, 1964. There were no Navy advisors in the production. Unable to laugh at themselves as described in the movie, the Navy discouraged the film's distribution at its bases. The producers did not even bother to ask the Navy for limited assistance for its D-Day landing sequence.[24]

23. *New York Times*, November 7, 1964.

24. *New York Times*, November 8, 1964.

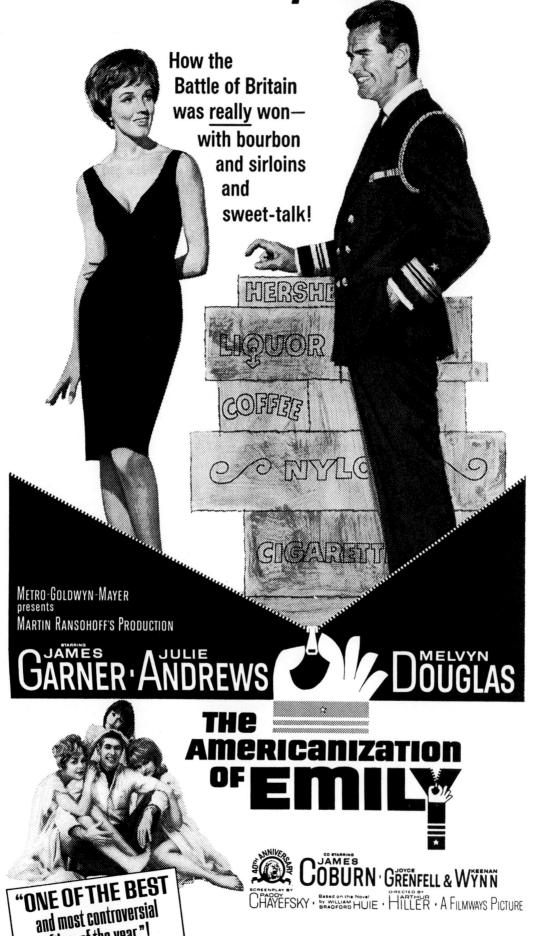

This is a story filled with romance, comedy, and action. Lt. Cmdr. Charles Madison (James Garner) is a "dog-robber" for an admiral (Melvyn Douglas). A "dog-robber" is a junior officer who arranges dinners, parties, and women for his superiors. It is his job to see that they get the very best. Madison is well prepared for this easy assignment because he was an assistant hotel manager in civilian life. He meets Emily Barham (Julie Andrews) who is an English motor-pool driver for the U.S. Navy. Having lost a husband, brother, and her father in the war, she vehemently disapproves of the work he does for the admiral. She objects to his philosophy of cowardice as well. He disapproves of her "widow heroics," yet they both fall madly in love.

This brief romance is interrupted when Admiral Jessup (Melvyn Douglas), a man in obvious mental decline, concludes that the Army's planned D-Day landing on the coast of France will so up-stage the Navy, that he fears Congress will scrap the fleet. In order to lift the Navy's prestige, he invents a novel PR scheme. He assigns Madison and Lt. Cmdr. "Bus" Cummings (James Coburn) to land with a naval demolition group on Omaha Beach with the first wave of the invasion. Their mission will be to let the world know that the first man to die in the invasion of Europe is an American sailor. To be placed on the exact spot where the unfortunate lad had fallen would be a Tomb for the Unknown Sailor. Madison, fearing that he might be that very sailor refuses to go, but changes his mind when "Bus" threatens a court-martial. Delighted when he finds out that the first assault group had already left England, he is horrified to find out that the invasion has been postponed because of the weather and that he and "Bus" will be among the first men to hit the beach. Madison tries to make a run for it after the landing, but is shot by "Bus" in the thigh and hit by cross-fire. To "Bus'" consternation, Madison is not killed and will not be the first American to die on D-Day. "Bus" utters in disgust: "Instead of a dead hero we've got a live coward."

Admiral Jessup is remorseful because he sent his best "dog-robber" on such a dangerous mission. He wants to send him back to Washington D.C. for a hero's welcome, but Madison, sticking to his philosophical guns, will have none of that and declines. Meanwhile Emily reverses herself away from Madison's pacifism and talks him into going back to the USA with the admiral where he will be viewed as a reluctant hero. Later he will marry Emily. She will give up her process of Americanization which in this movie means the short time in which she went along with Madison's principles on glory, war, and honor.

Emily Barham (Julie Andrews), who works for the U.S. Navy in England, and Lt. Cmdr. Charles Madison (James Garner) begin a love affair before the D-Day landing at Normandy, France.

James Garner plays the first sailor to land on D-Day.

James Coburn, right, observes what he thinks is the first Navy man (James Garner) killed on the beaches of Normandy in MGM's *The Americanization of Emily.*

ENSIGN PULVER

A mild anti-military message also comes through in the melodramatic farce, *Ensign Pulver.* This sequel to the very successful *Mr. Roberts* is about life on the same cargo ship Mr. Roberts served on. As mentioned before, Roberts had been transferred to a destroyer and was later killed in action. All the characters are the same, but are played by different actors. Because of the weakness of the story, the characters in *Ensign Pulver* lack the brightness of the original cast. With the exception of a few humorous scenes, this film does not have much going for it. This Warner Bros. production was previewed at the studio on February 20, 1964.

Ensign Pulver (Robert Walker) is a young officer aboard the cargo ship *Reluctant.* Basically mixed up and immature, he has a severe inferiority complex because his two older brothers have always commanded more respect than he. He feels crushed when no one in the crew can imagine that he is the perpetrator of a sling-shot hit on the hated captain's buttocks. What self-esteem he has left is lost when the captain (Burl Ives) catches him with six bottles of whiskey and makes him throw them overboard. The captain of this small vessel is a bitter old man who came to the Navy from the merchant marine. His sole goal in life is to rise in rank. He loathes the crew and they hate him back. Truly an unpleasant character, he is strict, cranky, and mean. For example, he denies radioman John Bruno (Tommy Sands) leave to attend his baby daughter's funeral. He won't give the crew liberty and is offended when anyone asks "please." Bruno tries to kill the captain with a gun taken from Pulver's room. Instead the old man falls overboard. Pulver reluctantly releases a raft and tries to save him. Both he and the captain are swept away in a storm and they land on a small island. There he spots Scotty (Millie Perkins), a nurse he had met before. Meanwhile, appendicitis strikes the captain. Luckily, Pulver, an avid reader of medical books, is prepared. Getting instructions from "Doc" (Walter Matthau) over the wireless, he performs a successful operation. The captain's explanation as to why he is so mean and gruff is not very convincing and this scrape with death has not changed him. When Pulver sees there is no hope for the captain to change his ways, he miraculously forces the old man to file transfer papers. There is merriment and celebration when the abrasive captain leaves the ship and Pulver gets what he most craves, adulation.

There was no cooperation between the Navy and the studio in this production. All naval type equipment used was rented from the Mexican Navy (Maritimos Mexicana). The cargo ship *Reluctant* was played by a former US Navy ship serving with the Mexican Navy under the name of *Colina*. She was pulled off the Manzanillo-Panama run and was completely refurbished by studio technicians. Two cabin cruisers, a motor launch, a speedboat, and a fishing boat converted into a YP "yippie" ship were also used. The Mexican government lent one of their C-47s as well.

The film company spent a month on location at Puerto Marques, eight miles from Acapulco. Shark activity caused the postponement of some of the water scenes and shark repellant was used around the dock area to keep sharks away while filming was going on. Palm trees had to be purchased at local nurseries when the film crew found out that the place they were filming, Pie de la Cuesta, did not have a single tree. About a week of filming was done off Catalina Island. There they filmed the lost at sea sequence that they could not film off of Acapulco. The scene where Pulver and the captain reach a friendly island was shot at Point Sequit, north of Malibu, California. The appendectomy episode that saved the captain's life was filmed on Stage 11 at the Warner Bros. Studios in Burbank.[25]

McHALE'S NAVY

McHale's Navy, an offshoot of the very popular television show was first reviewed on June 23, 1964. This hour and a half movie includes the same zany cast that appears in the series. McHale is the easy-going captain of *PT 73*. Pleasure and profit and not fighting a war is his top priority. Ensign Parker (Tim Conway) appears as one of the wildest junior officers the Navy ever had. With flawless timing, his slapstick antics are hilarious. His blundering escapades go beyond slapstick to the ridiculous. McHale's superior Captain Binghampton's (Joe Flynn) number one desire is to see McHale court-martialed. The rest of the crew helps to break every regulation and so it seems they are having a private war with the Navy. Even the Japanese are funny. McHale keeps

a Japanese POW as a cook (Yoshio Yoda). His Yiddish "oi veh" and Italian "mama mia" are not the kind of colloquialisms one expects to hear from a Japanese sailor. Even the Japanese submariners are funny in that they think a horse standing on a PT-Boat is a secret weapon.

In this episode, McHale's problems begin when he and his crew go into debt when their delayed horse racing scheme using an Australian track backfires and the favorite *Silver Spot* comes in first. Fear of marines breaking their heads over the payoff sends the PT-Boat to New Caledonia where McHale puts Lester Gruber (Carl Ballantine) at the gaming table to win the needed $2,000 quickly. When he fails, McHale tries to get it from the casino owner Margot Monet (Jean Willes), but this marriage-hungry women has a price. McHale must marry her.

The "feather brained" Ensign Parker gets the crew further in the hole when he crashes the PT boat into a warehouse owned by Henri Le Clerc (George Kennedy). Things begin to look up when they see *Silver Spot*, the great Australian horse, who swims away from a torpedoed freighter. If McHale can get this horse entered in the big horse race at New Caledonia on Bastille Day, he will be able to repay his debts. Binghampton has the goods on McHale, but is talked into being seasick when the horse is being taken to the race on a PT-Boat. Heading for the French Island, a Japanese sub stalks the craft believing that the horse standing astride the bow is a secret weapon. The horse is disguised with mattress hair, but near the finish line the hair falls off. McHale watching from his PT-Boat, orders a smoke-screen so that the race's finish will be obscured. At the same time the Japanese sub starts shelling the area and McHale rams his boat into the enemy sub and takes prisoners. Le Clerc, meanwhile, excuses the debt because McHale and the crew have saved the town from the enemy. But Parker rams the boat into the same warehouse again and McHale is in trouble once more. Margot may get her man yet!

Over 200 horses were interviewed to find the one that could stand easily as the PT-Boat moved through the water. Authenticity was a goal even in a raucous movie of this kind. A 17-building naval base complex of Quonset huts and recreation halls was built for $300,000. A jungle was erected on a ten-acre site. It included 24 forty-foot plastic palm trees with plastic coconuts. A lagoon from an earlier T.V. series was drained, deepened, and widened by a fleet of bulldozers to accommodate PT-boat facsimiles.[26]

25. Production File, *Ensign Pulver*, Academy of Motion Picture Arts and Sciences, Margaret Herrick Library, Beverly Hills, CA.

26. Universal Studios, *McHale's Navy* (For Your Information), March 13, 1964, pp. 2-3. Academy of Motion Picture Arts and Sciences. Margaret Herrick Library, Beverly Hills, CA.

EPILOGUE

The over forty movies about the United States Navy in World War II made in Hollywood between 1938 and 1976, to a large degree, mirror the attitudes and policies of the American nation during these momentous decades. With government encouragement and support, the movie industry reacted to Adolph Hitler's early aggressions by making two movies about German U-Boats which were clearly reminiscent of German "misdeeds" during the First World War. The motion picture *Sergeant York* in 1941 was the leading film that used the First World War to rekindle the past enmity between Germany and the United States. When it became obvious to all that air power was going to be a major factor in determining the course of the Second World War, Warner Bros. and MGM with strong government support produced three films about naval air power. Japan was clearly on the mind of the Navy when it opened its facilities in San Diego for the movie *Wings of the Navy* in 1938. This was also true about *Flight Command* in 1940 and *Dive Bomber* in 1941. The government's motive in assisting in the production of these movies was to inform the American people that the United States was not falling behind militarily; and that the recruitment of able young men for the naval air service was another objective. At the same time, the Navy encouraged Hollywood to make musicals and comedies to attract young men to recruiting stations. "Fun and girl" movies like *In the Navy* and *Navy Blues* just before the Pearl Harbor attack were entertaining and brought thousands of recruits into the Navy. Isolationist critics were no match for the combined strength of the United States government and the film industry.

When war came, Hollywood was at first unable to provide meaningful war films for the public and many of them were warmed over traditional Hollywood adventure stories and westerns. It was not until the release in early 1944 of *Destination Tokyo* that Hollywood produced a naval war film that was meticulously authentic and mindful of why the United States was at war. *They Were Expendable* coming out just as the war ended was another classic naval war film. They both portrayed the human side of the war and reflected the American determination to win that war. Though *The Fighting Sullivans* (1944) depicted little about

the Navy itself, it did portray American family values which were threatened by the rise of fascism.

After the Pearl Harbor debacle, Hollywood reflected the change in the nature of naval warfare and moved away from the battleship as the mainstay of the U.S. Navy and began depicting stories about destroyers, submarines and aircraft carriers. *Wing and a Prayer* (1944) demonstrated the role of the aircraft carrier in the Pacific War. *Task Force*, begun in 1944 and completed in 1949 showed the American people how "floating air fields" had won the Second World War and should continue their important role in the defense of the United States.

There was a massive increase in war films with the advent of the Cold War and the Korean War in the 1950s. Eight Hollywood feature films and numerous television programs about the activities of the American submarine force in the Second World War were shown during these years. It is probable that these films, encouraged by the Navy, helped to provide the public support needed for the construction of a large nuclear underseas fleet.

There were a number of reasons why Hollywood made fewer movies about the Navy in World War II in the 1960s. First of all the anti-war sentiment linked to the Viet Nam War was not conducive to making films about the military; secondly producers and directors who had experience with these types of films were leaving the scene. Finally, interest in domestic problems tended to deaden interest in this topic.

This is not to say that there were no other important movies about the Navy in World War II produced during this post-war period. *Tora! Tora! Tora!* (1970) reawakened American interest in the possibility that we could again one day be attacked not by dive bombers but by missiles. And *Midway* (1976), a highly successful film, reinforced the idea that the United States might have lost the Second World War if it were not for our "floating airfields."

Some of the best films about the Navy in the Second World War made in the post-war period were less propagandistic and self-serving. *The Caine Mutiny* (1954) and *Mr. Roberts* (1955) remain classics because they tell us about real men. *The Enemy Below* (1957) remains a well-thought-of film because adversarial confrontations are universal and the acting was superb.

SELECTED BIBLIOGRAPHY

Basinger, Jeanine. *The World War II Combat Film: Anatomy of a Genre*. New York Columbia University Press, 1986.

Bellamy, Ralph. *When the Smoke Hits the Fan*. New York: Doubleday & Company, 1979.

Dick, Bernard. *Star-Spangled Screen: The American Film in World War II*. Lexington: University of Kentucky Press, 1985.

Dolan, Edward F. *Hollywood Goes to War*. New York: Gallery Books, 1985.

Harrod, Frederick S. *The Manning of the New Navy: The Development of a Modern Naval Enlisted Force, 1899–1940*. Westport: Greenwood Press, 1978.

Hyams, Jay. *War Movies*. New York: Galley Books, 1984.

Isenberg, Michael T. *War on Films: The American Cinema in World War I, 1914-18*. London and Toronto: Farleigh Dickenson Press. 1981.

Langman, Michael T. and Borg, Ed. *Encyclopedia of American War Films*. New York: Garland Publishing, Inc., 1989.

Lorelli, John A. *The Battle of the Komandorski Islands*. Annapolis: Naval Institute Press, 1984.

Morison, Samuel E. *The Two Ocean War*. Boston: Little Brown and Company, 1963.

Orriss, Bruce W. *When Hollywood Ruled the Skies*. Hawthorne: Aero Associates, Inc., 1984.

Roscoe, Theodore. *United States Submarine Operations in World War II*, Annapolis: Naval Institute Press, 1949.

Shain, Russell E. *An Analysis of Motion Pictures About War Released by the American Film Industry*. New York: Arno Press, 1976.

Steele, Richard W. *Propaganda in an Open Society: The Roosevelt Administration and the Media*. Westport, Greenwood Press, 1986.

Suid, Lawrence H. *Guts and Glory: Great American War Movies*. Reading: Addison-Wesley Publishing Co., 1978.

Thomas, Tony. *Errol Flynn: The Spy Who Never Was*. New York: Citidal Press, 1990.

ORIGINAL SOURCES

Academy of Motion Picture Arts and Sciences, Margaret Herrick Library. Beverly Hills, California.

National Archives, Washington, D.C. Modern Military Records Division, Record Group 60 and 80.

Stanford University Special Collections Library, Stanford, California: Delmer Daves Papers.

UCLA Special Collections Library.

Warner Bros. Archives, University of Southern California.

PERIODICALS

Box Office Showmandiser
Christian Century
Cinema Texas Program Notes
Cue
Film Daily
Hollywood Citizen News
Hollywood Quarterly
Los Angeles Herald Express
Los Angeles Examiner
Los Angeles Mirror-News
Los Angeles Times
Motion Picture Herald
Newsweek
New York Herald Tribune
New York Times
New Statesman & Nation
New West
The Hollywood Reporter
Time
Toronto Film Society, Summer Series
Variety
University of Dayton Review

APPENDIX I
Major Studios' World War II Navy Films

COLUMBIA PICTURES
Submarine Patrol, 1942
Destroyer, 1943
Battle Stations, 1956
Hellcats of the Navy, 1957
Caine Mutiny, 1954

METRO-GOLDWYN-MAYER
Thunder Afloat, 1939
Flight Command, 1941
Stand by for Action, 1943
This Man's Navy, 1945
They Were Expendable, 1945
Torpedo Run, 1958
Wings of Eagles, 1957
Americanization of Emily, 1964

MONOGRAM
Flat Top, 1952

PARAMOUNT
The Fleet's In, 1942
Submarine Command, 1951
In Harm's Way, 1965
The Deep Six, 1957

REPUBLIC
Sailors on Leave, 1941
The Fighting Seabees, 1944
Torpedo Alley, 1952

RKO
The Navy Comes Through, 1942

UNITED ARTISTS
Run Silent, Run Deep, 1958
The Gallant Hours, 1960

UNIVERSAL INTERNATIONAL
In the Navy, 1941
Away All Boats, 1956
Operation Petticoat, 1959
McHale's Navy, 1964
Midway, 1976

TWENTIETH CENTURY FOX
Submarine Patrol, 1938
Sailor's Lady, 1940
Crash Dive, 1943
The Fighting Sullivans, 1944
The Enemy Below, 1957
Tora! Tora! Tora!, 1970

WARNER BROS.
Wings of the Navy, 1939
Dive Bomber, 1941
Navy Blues, 1941
Destination Tokyo, 1944
Task Force, 1949
Operation Pacific, 1951
Mr. Roberts, 1955
Up Periscope, 1959
PT 109, 1963
Ensign Pulver, 1964

APPENDIX II
Navy Ships Used in Hollywood Productions

PRODUCTION	SHIP	PRODUCTION	SHIP
Shipmates, 1932	USS *Colorado* (BB-45)	*Operation Petticoat*, 1959	USS *Baloa* (SS-285)
Here Comes the Navy, 1934	USS *Arizona* (BB-39)	*The Caine Mutiny*, 1954	USS *Thompson* (DMS-38)
Flight Command, 1940	USS *Enterprise* (CV-6)		USS *Doyle* (DMS-34)
Dive Bomber, 1941	USS *Enterprise* (CV-6)	*Mr. Roberts*, 1955	USS *Hewell* (AG-145)
Wing and a Prayer, 1944	USS *Yorktown* (CV-10)	*Away All Boats*, 1956	USS *Randall* (AP-224)
Task Force, 1949	USS *Antietam* (CV-36)	*In Harm's Way*, 1965	USS *St. Paul* (CA-73)
	USS *Bairoko* (CVE-115)		USS *Phillip* (DD-498)
Midway, 1976	USS *Lexington* (CV-AVT-16)	*The Wings of Eagles*, 1957	USS *Philippine Sea* (CV-48)
Flat Top, 1952	USS *Princeton* (CV-37)	*The Enemy Below*, 1957	USS *Whitehurst* (DE-534)
Battle Stations, 1956	USS *Princeton* (CV-37)	*The Deep Six*, 1958	USS *Stephen Potter* (DD-538)
Up Periscope, 1959	USS *Tilefish* (SS-307)	*Ensign Pulver*, 1964	M.M. *Colina* (Maritmos Mexicana)

"SAILORS ON LEAVE"

A REPUBLIC PICTURE

WILLIAM
LUNDIGAN
SHIRLEY
ROSS
CHICK CHANDLER
RUTH DONNELLY
MAE CLARKE
CLIFF NAZARRO
TOM KENNEDY
MARY AINSLEE
BILL SHIRLEY
JANE KEAN

Screen play by Art Arthur & Malcolm Stuart Boylan · Original story by Herbert Dalmas

DIRECTED BY ALBERT S. ROGELL

submarine
raider

Battling
Jap Treachery
On The Eve Of
Pearl Harbor!

with

JOHN HOWARD · MARGUERITE CHAPMAN
Bruce Bennett · Eileen O'Hearn · Larry Parks · Roger Clark
Original Screen play by Aubrey Wisberg · Produced by WALLACE MacDONALD
Directed by LEW LANDERS · A COLUMBIA PICTURE

PRINTED IN U.S.A.

ROBERT
TAYLOR
Flight
Command

"Take a deep breath, Hell Cat! You've been making love to your commander's wife!"

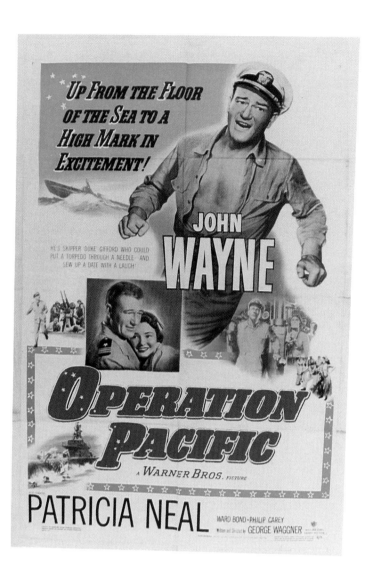

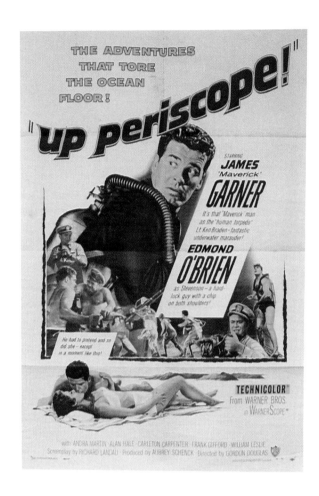

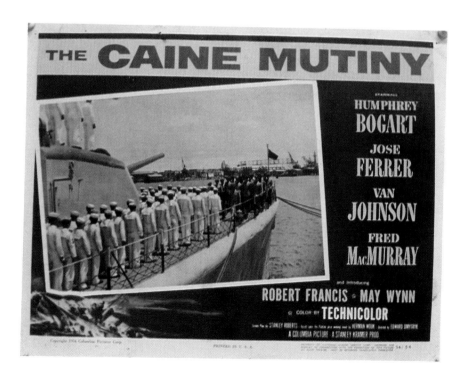

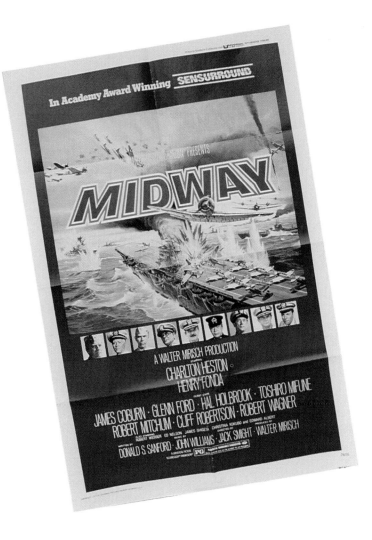

Robert Montgomery presents
James Cagney THE GALLANT HOURS
as Admiral Halsey

with DENNIS WEAVER · ROBERT MONTGOMERY · BERNIE LAY and FRANK GILROY
A CAGNEY-MONTGOMERY PRODUCTIONS, INC. Picture · Released thru UNITED ARTISTS

Copyright © 1960 United Artists Corporation. Country of Origin U.S.A.

The
story
of
a
band
of
men
left
for
dead
in
a
flaming
sea
and
their
epic
of
heroism
and
survival!

PT 109

starring CLIFF ROBERTSON

TY HARDIN · JAMES GREGORY · ROBERT CULP · GRANT WILLIAMS

A moment of triumph as "Spig" Wead (John Wayne) and his Navy crew celebrate.

M-G-M
Presents **"THE WINGS OF EAGLES"** in METROCOLOR

Copyright © 1957 Loew's Incorporated   COUNTRY OF ORIGIN U.S.A.   2

TORA!
TORA!
TORA!

FILM CREDITS

SUBMARINE PATROL
Twentieth Century Fox, 1938
CAST: Peter Townsend III: RICHARD GREENE; Susan Leeds: NANCY KELLY; Lt. John G. Drake: PRESTON FOSTER; Captain Leeds: GEORGE BANCROFT; Ellsworth "Spotts" Fickets: SLIM SUMMERVILLE; Anne: JOAN VALERIE; McAllison: JOHN CARRADINE; "Rocky" Hagerty: WARREN HYMER; Luigi: HENRY ARNETTA; Brett: DOUGLAS FAWLEY; "Sails": J. FARREL McDONALD; Johnny Miller: DICK HOGAN; Sgt. Joe Duffy: MAXI ROSENBLOOM; Olaf Swanson: WARD BOND
CREDITS: Director: JOHN FORD; Producer: DARRYL F. ZANUCK; Screenplay: BRIAN JAMES, DARRELL WARE, and JACK YELLEN; Original Story: JOHN MILHOLLAND; Photography: ARTHUR MILLER; Music Direction: ART LANGE; Film Editor: ROBERT SIMPSON; Art Director: WILLIAM DARLING and HANS PETERS; Set Direction: THOMAS PETERS

THUNDER AFLOAT
Metro-Goldwyn-Mayer, 1939
CAST: Jon Thorson: WALLACE BEERY; Susan Thorson: VIRGINIA GREY; Rocky Blake: CHESTER MORRIS. Other players are Douglas Dumbrille, Carl Esmond, Clem Bevans, John Qualen, Regis Toomey, Henry Victor, Addison Richards, Hans Joby, Henry Hunter, and Jonathan Hall
CREDITS: Director: GEORGE B. SEITZ; Producer: J. WALTER RUBEN; Screenplay: WELLS ROOT, Cmdr. HARVEY HAISLIP; Original Story: RALPH WHEELWRIGHT and Cmdr. HARVEY HAISLIP; Photography: JOHN F. SEITZ; Music Direction: WARD and DAVID SNELL; Film Editor: FRANK B. HULL; Art Direction: CEDRIC GIBBONS and URIE McCLEARY; Set Direction: EDWIN B. WILLIS

WINGS OF THE NAVY
Warner Bros., 1939
CAST: Cass Harrington: GEORGE BRENT; Irene Dale: OLIVIA DE HAVILLAND; Jerry Harrington: JOHN PAYNE; "Scat" Allen: FRANK McHUGH. Other players are John Litel, Victor Jory, Henry O'Neill, John Ridgely, John Gallaudet, Donald Briggs, Edgar Edwards, Regis Toomey, Albert Morin, Jonathan Hale, Pierre Watkin, Don Douglas, Max Hoffman, Alan Davis, and Larry Williams
CREDITS: Director: LLOYD BACON; Producer: HAL B. WALLIS; Original Screenplay: MICHAEL FESSIER; Photography: ARTHUR EDESON, ELMER DYER; Air Operations: PAUL MANTZ and FRANK CLARKE; Art Direction: EDRAS HARTLEY; Special Effects: HANS KOENKAMP; Film Editor: GEORGE AMY; Musical Director: LEO F. FORSTEIN

FLIGHT COMMAND
Metro-Goldwyn-Mayer, 1941
CAST: Alan Drake: ROBERT TAYLOR; Lorna Gary: RUTH HUSSEY; Bill Gary: WALTER PIDGEON; "Dusty" Rhodes: PAUL KELLY; Jerry Banning: SHEPPERD STRUDWICK; "Mugger" Martin: RED SKELTON; "Spike" Knowles: NAT PENDLETON. Other players are Dick Purcell, William Tanne, William Stelling, Stanley Smith, Addison Richards, Donald Douglas, Pat Flaherty, Forbes Murray, and Marsha Hunt
CREDITS: Director: FRANK BORZAGE; Producer: J. WALTER RUBEN; Screenplay: WELLS ROOTS and Cmdr. HARVEY HAISLIP, USN (Ret.); Original Story by: Cmdr. HARVEY HAISLIP and JOHN SUTHERLAND, USN; Technical Advisor: Cmdr. MORTON SELIGMAN, USN; Photography: HAROLD ROSSON, RICHARD ROSSON, and ELMER DYER; Air Operations: PAUL MANTZ, LAURA INGALLS, and FRANK CLARKE; Film Editor: ROBERT J. KERN; Music Director: FRANZ NEWMAN; Art Direction: CEDRIC GIBBONS; Set Director: EDWIN B. WILLIS; Special Effects: A. ARNOLD GILLESPIE

DIVE BOMBER
Warner Bros., 1941
CAST: Douglas Lee: ERROL FLYNN; Joe Blake: FRED MacMURRAY; Lance Rogers: RALPH BELLAMY; Linda Fisher: ALEXIS SMITH; Robert Armstrong: ART LYONS; Tim Griffin: REGIS TOOMEY; "Lucky" James: ALLEN JENKINS. Other players are Craig Stevens, Herbert Anderson, Moroni Olsen, Dennis Moore, Louis Jean Heydt, and Cliff Nazarro.
CREDITS: Director: MICHAEL CURTIZ; Producer: ROBERT LORD; Screenplay: FRANK W. WEAD and ROBERT BUCKNER; Original Story: FRANK W. WEAD and ROBERT BUCKNER; Photography: BERT CLEMMON and WINSTRON C. HOCK, ELMER DYER, and CHARLES A. MARSHALL; Air Operations: PAUL MANTZ; Film Editor: GEORGE AMY; Music Direction: MAX STEINER; Art Direction: ROBERT HASS; Special Effects: BYRON HASKIN and REX WIMPY

SAILOR'S LADY
Twentieth Century Fox, 1940
CAST: Danny Malone: JON HALL; Sally Gilroy: NANCY KELLY; Myrtle: JOAN DAVIS; Miss Purvis: MARY NASH; Scrappy Wilson: DANA ANDREWS; Rodney: LARRY "BUSTER" CRABBE; Georgine: KAY ALDRIDGE; Father McCann: HARRY SHANNON; Goofer: WALLY VERNON; "Skipper": BRUCE HAMPTON
CREDITS: Director: ALLAN DWAN; Producer: SOL WURTZEL; Screenwriter: FREDERICK HAZLETT

BRENNAN, LOU BRESLOW, and OWEN FRANCIS;
Original Story: FRANK W. WEAD; Photography:
ERNEST PALMER; Film Editor: FRED ALLEN; Musical
Director: SAMUEL KAYLIN; Technical Advisor: Lt.
Cmdr. A.J. BOLTON, USN

IN THE NAVY
Universal-International, 1941
C A S T : Smoky: BUD ABBOTT; Pomeroy Watson: LOU
COSTELLO; Tommy Halstead: DICK POWELL;
Dorothy Roberts: CLAIRE DODD; The Andrews Sisters:
THE ANDREWS SISTERS; Dynamite Dugan: DICK
FORAN; Butch: BILLY LENHARDT; Buddy:
KENNETH BROWN; Dizzy: SHEMP HOWARD
C R E D I T S : Director: ARTHUR LUBIN; Producer:
ALEX GOTTLIEB; Screenplay: ARTHUR T. HORMAN
and JOHN GRANT; Original Story: ARTHUR T.
HORMAN; Photography: JOSEPH VALENTINE; Film
Editor: PHILLIP CAHN; Special Effects: JOHN P.
FULTON; Technical Advisor: E.H. HARRIS, USN (Ret.)

NAVY BLUES
Warner Bros., 1941
C A S T : Margie Jordan: ANN SHERIDAN; Cake O'Hara:
JACK OAKIE; Liliebelle Bolton: MARTHA RAYE;
Powerhouse Bolton: JACK HALEY; Homer Mathews:
HERBERT ANDERSON; "Buttons" Johnson: JACK
CARSON; "Tubby": JACKIE GLEASON; "Rocky"
Anderson: RICHARD LANE: Mac: WILLIAM T.
MOORE; Navy Blues Sextet: PEGGY DIGGENS,
GEORGIA CARROLL, LORRAINE GETTMAN,
MARGUERITE CHAPMAN, KATHERINE
ALDRIDGE, and CLAIRE JAMES
C R E D I T S : Director: LLOYD BACON; Producer: HAL
WALLIS; Screenplay: JERRY WALD, RICHARD
McCAULY, ARTHUR HORMAN, SAM PERRIN;
Original Story: ARTHUR T. HORMAN; Photography:
TONY GAUDIO, JAMES WONG HOWE; Film Editor:
RUDY FEHR; Music Director: ARTHUR SCHWARTZ

SAILOR'S ON LEAVE
Republic, 1941
C A S T : Chuck Stephen: WILLIAM LUNDIGAN; Linda
Hall: SHIRLEY ROSS; "Swifty": CHICK CHANDLER;
Aunt Navy: RUTH DONNELLY; Gwen: MAE CLARK;
Mike: CLIFF NAZARRO. Other players are Tom
Kennedy, Mary Ainslee, Bill Shirley, Gary Own, William
Haade, and Joan Kean
C R E D I T S : Director: ALBERT S. NOGELL; Producer:
ALBERT J. COHEN; Screenwriter: ART ARTHUR and
MALCOLM S. BOYALN; Original Story: HERBERT
DALMAS; Photography: ERNEST MILLER; Film Editor:
EDWARD MANN; Music and Lyrics: JULES STYNE and
FRANK LOESSER

THE FLEET'S IN
Paramount, 1942
C A S T : "The Countess": DOROTHY LAMOUR; Casey
Kirby: WILLIAM HOLDEN; Barney Waters: EDDIE
BRACKEN; Bessie Day: BETTY HUTTON; Cissy: CASS
DALEY; Spike: GIL LAMB; Jake: LEIF ERICKSON;
JIMMY DORSEY and his Orchestra, featuring Helen
O'Connell and Bob Eberle
C R E D I T S : Director: VICTOR SCHERTZINGER;
Producer: PAUL JONES; Screenwriters: WALTER DE
LEON, RALPH SPENCE, SID SILVERS; Original Story:
MONTE BRYCE and J. WALTER RUBEN; Photography:
WILLIAM MELLOR; Film Editor: PAUL
WEATHERWAX

SUBMARINE RAIDER
Columbia, 1942
C A S T : Submarine Commander: JOHN HOWARD; Sue
Curry: MARGUERITE CHAPMAN; First Officer:
BRUCE BENNET; Captain Yamada: NINO PEPITONE.
Other players: Japanese Officer: KEY LUKE
C R E D I T S : Director: LEW LANDERS; Producer:
WALLACE MacDONALD; Screenplay: AUBREY
WISBERG; Photography: FRANK BENTLEY

THE NAVY COMES THROUGH
RKO, 1942
C A S T : Mallory: PAT O'BRIEN; Sands: GEORGE
MURPHY; Myra: JANE WYATT; Babe: JACKIE
COOPER; Kroner: CARL ESMOND; Berringer: MAX
BAER; Tarriba: DESI ARNAZ; Young German Sailor:
HELMIT DANTINE
C R E D I T S : Director: A. EDWARD SUTHFRLAND;
Producer: ISLEN AUSTIER; Screenwriters: RAY
CHANSLOR, EARL BALDWIN, JOHN TWIST;
Original Story: BORDEN CHASE; Photography:
NICHOLAS MUSURACA; Film Editor: SAMUEL E.
BEETLEY; Musical Director: C. BAKALEINIKOFF; Art
Director: ALBERT S. D'AGOSTINO and CARROL
CLARK; Special Effects: VERNON L. WALKER

STAND BY FOR ACTION
Metro-Goldwyn-Mayer, 1943
C A S T : Lt. Greg Masterman: ROBERT TAYLOR;
Admiral Stephen Thomas: CHARLES LAUGHTON; Lt.
Cmdr. Martin Roberts: BRIAN DONLEVY; Chief
Yeoman Henry Johnson: WALTER BRENNAN. Other
players are Marilyn Maxwell, Henry O'Neill, Marta
Linden, and Chill Wills
C R E D I T S : Directors: ROBERT Z. LEONARD and
ORVILL O. DULL; Producer: ROBERT Z. LEONARD
and ORVILLE C. DULL; Screenwriters: GEORGE
BRUCE, JOHN L. BALDTERSTON, and HERMAN
MANCIEWICZ; Original Story: LAWRENCE KIRK;
Photography: CHARLES ROSHER; Music Direction:
LENNIE HAYTON; Film Editor: GEORGE BOEMLER;
Art Director: CEDRIC GIBBONS; Special Effects:

A. ARNOLD GILLESPIE and DON JAHRAUS;
Technical Advisor: Lt. Cmdr. H.D. SMITH, USN

CRASH DIVE
Twentieth Century Fox, 1943
CAST: Lt. Ward Stewart: TYRONE POWER; Jean
Hewlett: ANNE BAXTER; Cmdr. Dewey Connors:
DANA ANDREWS; McDonnell: JAMES GLEASON;
Grandmother: DAME MAY WHITTY; Brownie: HENRY
MORGAN; Oliver Cromwell Jones: BEN CARTER
CREDITS: Director: ARCHIE MAYO; Producer:
MILTON SPERLING; Screenwriter: JO SWERLING JR.;
Original Story: W.R. BURNETT; Photography: LEON
SHAMROY (Technicolor); Music: DAVID BUTTOLPH;
Music Direction: EMIL NEWMAN; Film Editor:
WALTER THOMPSON and RAY CURTIS; Art
Direction: RICHARD DAY and WIARD IHNEN; Set
Direction: PAUL FOX and THOMAS LITTLE; Special
Effects: FRED SERSEN

DESTROYER
Columbia, 1943
CAST: Steve Boleslavski: EDWARD G. ROBINSON;
Mickey Donohue: GLENN FORD; Mary Boleslavski:
MARGUERITE CHAPMAN; "Kansas" Jackson: EDGAR
BUCHANAN; Sarecky: LEO GORCEY; Lt. Cmdr. Clark:
REGIS TOOMEY; Casey: ED BROPHY; Lt. Morton:
WARREN ASCHE; Bigbee: CRAIG WOODS; Yash:
CURT BOIS
CREDITS: Director: WILLIAM SEITER; Producer:
LOUIS F. EDELMAN; Screenwriter: FRANK W. WEAD,
LEWIS MEIZER, and BORDON CHASE; Original
Story: FRANK W. WEAD; Photography: FRANZ F.
PLANER; Film Editor: GENE HAVLICK; Music
Direction: M.W. STOLOFF; Art Direction: LIONEL
BANKS

DESTINATION TOKYO
Warner Bros., 1944
CAST: Cmdr. Cassidy: CARY GRANT; Wolf: JOHN
GARFIELD; "Cookie": ALAN HALE; Raymond: JOHN
RIDGELY; "Tin Can": DANE CLARK; "Pills": WILLIAM
PRINCE; Tommy Adams: ROBERT HUTTON; Mike:
TOM TULLY; "Sparks": JOHN FORSYTHE
CREDITS: Director: DELMER DAVES; Producer:
JERRY WALD; Screenwriter: ALBERT MANTZ and
DELMER DAVES; Original Story: STEVEN FISHER;
Photography: BERT GLENNON; Music Direction: LEO
F. FORBSTEIN; Film Editor: CHARLES NYBY; Art
Direction: LEO K. KUTER; Set Direction: WALTER
TILFORD; Special Effects: LAWRENCE BUTLER and
WILLARD VAN ENGER; Technical Advisors: Lt. Cmdr.
PHILLIP COMPTON, USN, and Lt. Cmdr. D.W.
MORTON, USN; Chief Machinist Mate: ANDREW
LENNOX, USN

THE FIGHTING SEABEES
Republic Pictures, 1944
CAST: Wedge Donovan: JOHN WAYNE; Constance
Chelsey: SUSAN HAYWARD; Lt. Cmdr. Bob Yarrow:
DENNIS O'KEEFE. Other players are William Frawley,
Leonid Kinsky, J.M. Kerrigan, Grant Withers, Paul Fix, Ben
Welden, William Forrest, Addison Richards, Jay Norris,
and Duncan Renaldo
CREDITS: Director: EDWARD LUDWIG and
HOWARD HYDECKER; Producer: ALBERT J.
COHEN; Screenwriter: BORDEN CHASE and AENEAS
MACKENZIE; Original Story: BORDEN CHASE;
Photography: WILLIAM BRADFORD; Music Direction:
WALTER SCHARF; Film Editor: RICHARD VAN
ENGER; Art Director: DUNCAN CRAMER; Special
Effects: THEODORE LYDECKER

WING AND A PRAYER
Twentieth Century Fox, 1944
CAST: Bingo Harper: DON AMECHE; Moulton:
DANA ANDREWS; Oscar Scott: WILLIAM EYTHE;
Beezy Bessemer: RICHARD JAECKEL; Captain Waddell:
CHARLES BICKFORD; the Admiral: SIR CEDRIC
HARDWICKE. Other players are Kevin O'Shea, Henry
Morgan, Richard Crane, Glenn Langan, Renny McEvey,
Robert Bailey, Reed Hadley, George Mathews, B.S. Pully,
Dave Willock, Murray Alper, Charles Land and John Miles
CREDITS: Director: HENRY HATHAWAY; Producer:
WALTER MOROSCO, WILLIAM BACHER; Screenplay:
JEROME CADY; Photography: GLEN MacWILLIAMS;
Art Director: LEWIS CREBER and LYLE WHEELER; Set
Direction: THOMAS LITTLE and FRED RODE; Special
Effects: FRED SERSEN; Film Editor: WATSON WEBB;
Music Direction: HUGO FRIEDHOFER

THE FIGHTING SULLIVANS
Twentieth Century Fox, 1944
CAST: Mary Katherine: ANNE BAXTER; Mr. Sullivan:
THOMAS MITCHELL; Mrs. Sullivan: SELENA ROYLE;
Al: EDWARD RYAN; Genevieve: TRUDY MARSHALL;
Frank: JOHN CAMPBELL; George: JAMES
CARDWELL; Matt: JOHN ALVIN; Joe: GEORGE
OFFERMAN, JR., The Lieutenant: WARD BOND. As
children: Al: BOBBY DRISCOLL; Genevieve: JUNE
ROBINSON; Joe: JOHNNY CALKINS. Other players
are Jorn Nesbitt, Selmer Jackson, Roy Roberts, Mary
McCarty, Harry Shannon, Barbara Brown, Larry
Thompson, and Addison Richards
CREDITS: Director: LLOYD BACON; Producer: SAM
JAFFE; Screenwriter: MARY C. McCALL JR.; Original
Story: EDWARD DOHERTY and JULES SCHERMER;
Photography: LUCINE ANDROIT; Film Editor: LOUIS
LOEFFIER; Music Director: ALFRED NEWMAN; Art
Director: JAMES BASEVI and LELAND FULLER;
Special Effects: FRED SERSEN

THIS MAN'S NAVY

Metro-Goldwyn-Mayer, 1944

CAST: Ned Trumpet: WALLACE BEERY; CPO Shannon: JAMES GLEASON; Jess Weaver: TOM DRAKE; Catherine Cortland: JAN CLAYTON; Tim Shannon: STEVEN BRODIE; Chief Rigger: NOAH BEERY SR. Supporting players are George Chandler, Arthur Walsh, Paul Langton, Bill Phillips, Robert Sully, Selena Royle, Henry O'Neill, Frank Fenton, Reginald Owen, Bruce Kellogg

CREDITS: Director: WILLIAM WELLMAN; Producer: SAMUEL MARX; Screenwriters: JOHN TWIST, HUGH ALL, and ALLEN RIVKIN; Original Story: BURTON CHASE; Photography: SIDNEY WAGNER; Music Direction: NATHANIEL SHILRET; Film Editor: IRVINE WARBURTON; Art Direction: CEDRIC GIBBONS, HOWARD CAMPBELL; Set Direction: EDWIN B. WILLIS, GLEN BARNER; Special Effects: A. ARNOLD GILLESPIE and DONALD JAHRAUS

THE STORY OF DR. WASSELL

Paramount, 1944

CAST: Dr. Corydon W. Wassell: GARY COOPER; Madeline: LARAINE DAY; Bettina: SIGNE HASSO; Hopkins "Hoppy": DENNIS O'KEEFE; Tremartini: CAROL THURSTON; Lt. Dirk Van Daal: CARL ESMOND; Murdock: PAUL KELLY; Anderson (Andy): ELLIOT REID; Cmdr. Bill Goggins: STANLEY RIDGES. Other players are Renny McEvoy, Oliver Thorndike, Philip Ahn, Barbara Britton, Joel Allen, James Millican, Melvin Francis, Mike Killian, Doodles Weaver

CREDITS: Director: CECIL B. DeMILLE; Producer: CECIL B. DeMILLE; Screenplay: ALAN LEMAY and CHARLES BENNETT; Photography: VICTOR MILNER and WILLIAM SNYDER; Editor: ANNE BAUCHENS; Art Director: HANS DREIER and ROLAND ANDERSON; Sound: HUGO GRENZGBACK and JOHN COPE; Set Direction: GEORGE SAWLEY; Music: VICTOR YOUNG

ANCHORS AWEIGH

MGM, 1945

CAST: Joseph Brady: GENE KELLY; Susan Abbott: KATHRYN GRAYSON; Clarence Doolittle: FRANK SINATRA; Jose Iturbi: JOSE ITURBI; Donald Martin: DEAN STOCKWELL; Girl from Brooklyn: PAMELA BRITTON. Other players are Rags Ragland, Billy Gilbert, Carlos Ramirez, James Flavin and Edgar Kennedy

CREDITS: Director: GEORGE SIDNEY; Producer: JOE PASTERNAK; Screenplay: ISOBEL LENNART; Photography: ROBERT PLANCK and CHARLES BOYLE; Editor: ADRIENNE FAZAN; Animation Direction: WILLIAM HANNA and JOSEPH BARBERA; Choreography: GENE KELLY; Music: GEORGE STOLL; Song by: SAMMY CAHN and JULIE STYNE

THEY WERE EXPENDABLE

Metro-Goldwyn-Mayer, 1945

CAST: Lt. John Brinkley: ROBERT MONTGOMERY; Lt. "Rusty" Ryan: JOHN WAYNE; Lt. Sandy Davyss: DONNA REED; General Marshall: JACK HOLT: "Boats" Mulcahey: WARD BOND; Ens. Andy Andrews: PAUL LANGSTON; Ens. "Snake" Gardener: MARSHALL THOMPSON; Maj. James Morton: LEON AMES. Other players are Arthur Walsh, Donald Curtiss, Cameron Mitchell, Jeff York, Murray Alper, Harry Tenbrook, Jack Pennick, John Havier, Vernon Shields, Charles Tombridge, Robert Barrat, Bruce Kellogg, Tim Murdock, Louis Jean Heydt, Russell Simpson

CREDITS: Director: JOHN FORD, ROBERT MONTGOMERY; Producer: JOHN FORD; Photography: JOSEPH H. AUGUST; Music Direction: HERBERT STOHERT; Film Editor: FRANK E. HULL and MALCOLM F. BROWN; Set Direction: EDWIN B. WILLIS, RALPH S. HURST; Special Effects: A. ARNOLD GILLESPIE

TASK FORCE

Warner Bros., 1949

CAST: Jonathan L. Scott: GARY COOPER; Mary Morgan: JANE WYATT; McKinney: WAYNE MORRIS; Pete Richard: WALTER BRENNAN; Barbara McKinney: JULIE LONDON; McClusky: BRUCE BENNETT; Adm. Reeves: JACK HOLT. Other players are Stanley Ridges, Richard Robes, Art Baker

CREDITS: Director: DELMER DAVES; Producer: JERRY WALD; Screenwriter: DELMER DAVES; Photography: ROBERT BURKS, WILFRED M. CLINE; Music Direction: FRANZ WAXMAN; Film Editor: ALLAN CROSSLAND; Art Direction: LEO KUTER; Air Operations: PAUL MANTZ; Set Direction: GEORGE J. HOPKINS; Special Effects: ROY DAVIDSON and EDWIN du PAR; Sound: CHARLES LANG

OPERATION PACIFIC

Warner Bros., 1951

CAST: Duke Gifford: JOHN WAYNE; Mary Stuart: PATRICIA NEAL; "Pop": WARD BOND. Other players are Scott Forbes, Philip Carey, Paul Picerni, Bill Campbell, Jack Pennick, Virginia Brissas, Vincent Fote, Lewis Martin, Louis Mosconi, and Sam Edwards

CREDITS: Director: GEORGE WAGGNER; Producer: LOUIS F. EDELMAN; Screenwriter: GEORGE WAGGNER; Photography: BERT GLENNON; Music Director: MAX STEINER; Art Director: LEO K. KUTER; Film Editor: ALAN CROSLAND; Technical Advisor: Adm. CHARLES A. LOCKWOOD, USN

SUBMARINE COMMAND
Paramount, 1951
CREDITS: Cmdr. Ken White: WILLIAM HOLDEN;
Lt. Cmdr. Peter Morris: DON TAYLOR; Chief Boyer:
WILLIAM BENDIX; Carol White: NANCY OLSON; Lt.
Barton: JACK KELLY; Mrs. Alice White: PEGGY
WEBBER; Adm. Rice: MARONI OLSEN
CREDITS: Director: JOHN FARROW; Producer:
JOSEPH SISTROM; Screenplay: JONATHAN
LATIMER; Photography: LIONEL LINDEN; Film
Editor: EDA WARREN; Music Direction: DAVID
BUTTOLPH; Art Direction: HAL PEREIRA and
HENRY BUMSTEAD; Technical Advisor: Rear Adm.
THOMAS DYKER, USN

FLAT TOP
Monogram Pictures, 1952
CAST: Dan Collier: STERLING HAYDEN; Joe
Rodgers: RICHARD CARLSON; Red Kelley: BILL
PHIPPS; Snakeships MacKay: JOHN BROMFIELD;
Barney Smith: KEITH LARSEN; Longfellow: WILLIAM
SCHALIERT; Commander: WALTER COY
CREDITS: Director: LESLEY SELANDER; Producer:
WALTER MIRISCH; Screenplay: STEVE FISHER; Special
Effects: HARRY COSWICK; Film Editor: WILLIAM
AUSTIN; Music Direction: MARLIN SKILES

TORPEDO ALLEY
Republic Pictures, 1952
CAST: Bob Bingham: MARK STEVENS; Susan Peabody:
DOROTHY MALONE; Warrant Officer Peabody:
CHARLES WINNINGER; Lt. Graham: BILL
WILLIAMS; Lt. Gates: DOUGLAS KENNEDY; Skipper:
JAMES SEAY
CREDITS: Director: LEW LANDERS; Producer:
LINDSLEY PARSONS; Screenplay: SAM ROECA,
WARREN DOUGLAS; Photography: WILLIAM
SICKNER; Film Editor: W. DONN HAYES; Art
Direction: DAVID MILTON; Technical Advisor:
Cmdr. B.R. VAN BUSKIRK, USN (Ret.) and Rear Adm.
THOMAS M. DYKERS, USN (Ret.)

THE CAINE MUTINY
Columbia Pictures, 1954
CAST: Cmdr. Philip Queeg: HUMPHREY BOGART;
Lt. Steven Maryk: VAN JOHNSON; Lt. Thomas Keefer:
FRED MacMURRAY; Lt. Barney Greenwald: JOSE
FERRER; Judge Advocate Challee: E.G. MARSHALL;
Ens. Willis Keith: ROBERT FRANCIS; Captain De Vriess:
TOM TULLY; Ens. Harding: JERRY PARIS; May Winn:
MAY WINN; "Meatball": LEE MARVIN; "Horrible":
CLAUDE AKINS. Other players are James Edwards,
Arthur Franz, Whit Bissel, Tod Karns, Herbert Anderson,
James Best, Dan Dubbins, Joe Haworth, Katherine Warren,
Steven Brodie, and Kenneth MacDonald.
CREDITS: Director: EDWARD DMYTRYK; Producer:
STANLEY KRAMER; Screenplay: STANLEY ROBERTS

and MICHAEL BLANKFORT; Photography: FRANK
PLANER; Film Editors: WILLIAM LYON and HENRY
BATISTA; Art Direction: GARY ODELL; Set Direction:
FRANK TUTTLE; Music Direction: MAX STEINER;
Technical Advisor: Cmdr. JAMES SHAW, USN

MR. ROBERTS
Warner Bros., 1955
CAST: Lt. Roberts: HENRY FONDA; Captain: JAMES
CAGNEY; Ens. Frank Pulver: JACK LEMMON; "Doc":
WILLIAM POWELL; CPO Dowdy: WARD BOND;
Lt. Anne Girard: BETSY PALMER. Other players are Phil
Carey, Nick Adams, Harry Carey Jr., Ken Curtis, Frank
Aletter, Friz Ford, Buck Kartalian, William Henry, William
Hudson, Stubby Krueger, Henry Tembrook, Pat Wayne,
Tige Andrews, and Jack Pennick
CREDITS: Directors: JOHN FORD, MERVYN LeROY
and JOSHUA LOGAN; Producer: LELAND HAY-
WARD; Screenplay: FRANK NUGENT and JOSEPH
LOGAN; Original Story: THOMAS HEGGEN;
Photography: WINTON HOCH; Film Editor: JACK
MURRAY; Art Direction: ART LOEL; Set Direction:
WILLIAM L. KUEHL; Music Direction: FRANZ
WAXMAN; Technical Advisors: Adm. JOHN DALE
PRICE, USN, and Cmdr. MERLE McBAIN, USN

AWAY ALL BOATS
Universal-International, 1956
CAST: Captain Jedidiah S. Hawks: JEFF CHANDLER;
Lt. Dave MacDougal: GEORGE NADER; Nadine
MacDougal: JULIE ADAMS; Cmdr. Quigley: LEX
BARKER; Dr. Bell: KEITH ANDES; Lt. Fraser:
RICHARD BOONE; Ens. Kruger: WILLIAM
REYNOLDS; Lt. O'Banion: CHARLES McGRAW;
Alvick: JACK MAHONEY; The Old Man: JOHN
McINTIRE
CREDITS: Director: JOSEPH PEVNEY; Producer:
HOWARD CHRISTIE; Screenplay: TED SHERDIMAN;
Original Story: KENNETH DODSON; Photography:
WILLIAM DANIELS, WILLIAM STINE; Film Editor:
TED KENT; Technicolor: WILLIAM FRITZSCE; Art
Direction: ALEXANDER GOLITZEN and RICHARD
RIEDEL; Set Direction: RUSSELL GAUSMAN and
OLIVER EMERT; Music Direction: JOSEPH GERSHEN-
SON; Sound Coordinators: LESLIE CAREY and JOE
LAPIS; Technical Advisors: Cpt. RICHARD GREGORY,
USN, and Cpt. ROBERT THEOBOLD, USN

BATTLE STATIONS
Columbia Pictures, 1956
CAST: Father Joe McIntyre: JOHN LUND; Buck
Fitzpatrick: WILLIAM BENDIX; Chris Jordan: KEEFE
BRASSELLE; Captain: RICHARD BOONE; Peter Kelly:
WILLIAM LESLIE. Other players are John Craven, James
Lyndon, Claude Akins, George O'Hanion, Eddie Foy III,
Jack Diamond, Chris Randall, Robert Forrest, Dick
Cathcart, Gordon Howard, James Librun, Fred Bund.

CREDITS: Director: LEWIS SEILER; Producer:
BRYAN FOY; Screenplay: CRANE WILBER; Original
Story: BEN FINNEY; Photography: BURNET GUFFY;
Film Editor: JEROME THOMAS; Music Direction:
MISCHA BAKALEINKOFF

THE DEEP SIX
Paramount Pictures, 1958
CAST: Lt. Alec Austen: ALAN LADD; Susan Cahill:
DIANNE FOSTER; "Frenchy" Shapiro: WILLIAM
BENDIX; Lt. Cmdr. Edge: KEENAN WYNN; Cmdr.
Meredith: JAMES WHITMORE; Lt. Blanchard: EFREM
ZIMBALIST JR.; Ski Krakowski: JOEY BISHOP. Other
players are the officers and men of the U.S.S. *Stephen Foster*
(DD-538)
CREDITS: Director: RUDOLPH MATE; Producer:
MARTIN RACKIN; Screenplay: JOHN TWIST,
MARTIN RACKIN, HARRY BROWN; Original Story:
MARTIN DIBNER; Photography: JOHN SEITZ (Warner
Color); Art Direction: LEO K. KUTER; Film Editor:
ROLAND GROSS; Sound: FRANCIS STAHL; Music
Direction: DAVID BUTTOLPH; Technical Advisor: Capt.
ALAN BROWN, USN

THE ENEMY BELOW
Twentieth Century Fox, 1957
CAST: Cmdr. Murrell: ROBERT MITCHUM; Von
Stolberg: CURT JURGENS; Lt. Ware: AL (DAVID)
HEDISON; Schwaffer: THEODORE BIKEL; Doctor:
RUSSELL COLLINS; Von Holem: KURT KRUGER; Ens.
Merry: DOUG McCLURE
CREDITS: Director: DICK POWELL; Producer: DICK
POWELL; Screenplay: WENDELL MAYES; Original
Story: Cmdr. D.A. RAYNOR, R.N.; Photography:
HAROLD ROSSON; Film Editor: STUART GILMORE;
Music Direction: LIONELL NEWMAN; Special Effects:
L.B. ABBOTT, WALTER ROSSI; Technical Advisors:
Lt. Cmdr. CHARLES E. DUNSTON, USN; Lt. Cmdr.
WALTER R. SMITH, USN; ALBERT BECK, a survivor
of four U-Boat sinkings

HELLCATS OF THE NAVY
Columbia Pictures, 1957
CAST: Cmdr. Casey Abbott: RONALD REAGAN;
Helen: NANCY DAVIS; Lt. Cmdr. Landon: ARTHUR
FRANZ; Lt. Baron: HARRY LAUTER. Other players are
Robert Arthur, William Leslie, William Phillips, Michael
Garth, Joseph Turkel, Don Keefer
CREDITS: Director: NATHAN JURAN; Producer:
CHARLES N. SCHNEER; Screenplay: DAVID LANG;
Original Story: CHARLES A. LOCKWOOD; Photog-
raphy: IRVING LIPPMAN; Film Editor: JEROME
THOMS; Art Direction: RUDI FELD; Technical Advisor:
Lt. Cmdr. WILLIAM R. BOOSE, USN

WINGS OF EAGLES
Metro-Goldwyn-Mayer, 1957
CAST: "Spig" Wead: JOHN WAYNE; Minnie Wead:
MAUREEN O'HARA; Carson: DAN DAILEY; John
Dodge: WARD BOND; John Dale Price: KEN CURTIS;
Adm. Moffett: EDMUND LOWE; Herbert Alan Hazard:
KENNETH TOBEY; James Todd: JACK TRAVIS; Capt.
Jock Clark: BARRY KELLY; The "Manager": SIG
RUMANN; Capt. Spear: HENRY O'NEAL; Barton:
WILLIS BOUCHEY; Rose Brentmann: DOROTHY
JORDAN; Pincus: TIGE ANDREWS
CREDITS: Director: JOHN FORD; Producer:
CHARLES SCHNEE; Screenplay: FRANK FENTON
and WILLIAM WIESTER HAINES; Photography (in
Metrocolor): PAUL E. VOGEL; Art Direction: WILLIAM
A. HORNING, MALCOLM BROWN; Set Direction:
EDWIN B. WILLIS and KEOGH GLEASON; Film
Editor: GENE RUGIERIO; Music Direction: JEFF
ALEXANDER; Aerial Stunts: PAUL MANTZ; Technical
Advisor: Adm. JOHN D. PRICE, USN (Ret.)

RUN SILENT, RUN DEEP
United Artists, 1958
CAST: Cmdr. Richardson: CLARK GABLE; Lt. Jim
Bledsoe: BURT LANCASTER; Mueller: JACK
WARDEN; Cartwright: BRAD DEXTER; Ruby: DON
RICKLES; Russo: NICK CRAVAT; Kohler: JOE
MOROSS; Laura: MARY LaROCHE; Larto: EDDIE
FOY III.
CREDITS: Director: ROBERT WISE; Producer:
HAROLD HECHT; Screenplay: JOHN GAY; Original
Story: EDWARD L. BEACH; Film Editor: GEORGE
BOEMLER; Art Direction: EDWARD CARRERE; Special
Effects: A. ARNOLD GILLESPIE; Technical Advisor:
Rear Adm. BOB McGREGOR, USN

TORPEDO RUN
Metro-Goldwyn-Mayer, 1958
CAST: Cmdr. Barney Doyle: GLENN FORD; Lt.
Archer Sloan: ERNEST BORGNINE; Jane Doyle:
DIANE BREWSTER; Lt. Jake "Fuzz" Foley: DEAN
JONES; "Hash" Benson: L.Q. JONES; Adm. Samuel
Setton: PHILLIP OBER; Lt. Don Adams: RICHARD
CARLYLE. Other players are Fred Wayne, Don Keefer,
Robert Hardy, and Paul Picerni.
CREDITS: Director: JOSEPH PEVNEY; Producer:
EDMOND GRAINGER; Screenplay: RICHARD SALE,
WILLIAM WISTER HAINE; Original Story: RICHARD
SALE; Photography: GEORGE FOLSEY; Film Editor:
GENE RUGGIERO; Art Direction: WILLIAM A.
HORNING and MALCOLM BROWN; Special Effects:
A. ARNOLD GILLESPIE; Technical Advisor: Vice Adm.
CHARLES A. LOCKWOOD, USN (Ret.)

OPERATION PETTICOAT
Universal Pictures, 1959
CREDITS: Cmdr. Matt Sherman: CARY GRANT; Lt. Nick Holden: TONY CURTIS; Lt. Delores Crandall: JOAN O'BRIEN; Lt. Barbara Duran: DINA MERRILL; Chief Tostin: ARTHUR O'CONNELL; McLumphery: GENE EVANS; Stovall: RICHARD SARGENT; Maj. Edna Hayward: VIRGINIA GREGG. Other players are Robert F. Simon, Robert Gist, Gavin McLeod, George Dunn, Dick Crockett, Madilyn Rhue, Marion Ross, Clarence E. Lung, Frankie Darro, Tony Pastor Jr., Robert Hay, Nicky Blair, and John Morley.
CREDITS: Director: BLAKE EDWARDS; Producer: ROBERT ARTHUR; Screenplay: STANLEY SHAPIRO and MAURICE RICHLIN; Original Story: PAUL KING and JOSEPH KING; Film Editor: TED J. KENT, FRANK GROSS; Photography: RUSSELL HARLAN; Art Direction: ALEX GOLITZEN and ROBERT E. SMITH; Music: DAVID ROSE

UP PERISCOPE
Warner Bros., 1959
CAST: Lt. (jg) Ken Braden: JAMES GARNER; Sally Johnson: ANDRA MARTIN; Cmdr. Stevenson: EDMOND O'BRIEN; Ens. Pat Malone: ALAN HALE; Lt. Phil Carny: CARLETON CARPENTER. Other players are Frank Gifford, William Leslie, Richard Bakalyan, Edward Byrnes, Sean Garrison, and Henry Kulky
CREDITS: Director: GORDON DOUGLAS; Producer: AUBREY SCHENK; Screenplay: RICHARD LANDAU; Original Story: ROBB SMITH; Photography: CARL GUTHRIE; Film Editor: JOHN SCHREYER; Art Direction: JACK T. COLLIS; Set Director: WILLIAM WALLACE; Music Direction: RAY HEINDORF

THE GALLANT HOURS
United Artists, 1960
CAST: Admiral William F. Halsey Jr.: JAMES CAGNEY; Lt. Cmdr. Andy Lowe: DENNIS WEAVER; Capt. Harry Black: WARD COSTELLO; Lt. Cmdr. Roy Webb: RICHARD JAECKEL; Capt. Frank Enright: LES TREMAYNE; Maj. Gen. Roy Geiger: RICHARD BURTON; Maj. Gen. Archie Vandergrift: RAYMOND BAILEY; Adm. Ghormley: CARL BENTON REID; Adm. Isoruku Yamamoto: JAMES T. GOTO; Rear Adm. Jiro Kobe: JAMES YAGI
CREDITS: Director: ROBERT MONTGOMERY; Producer: ROBERT MONTGOMERY; Screenplay: BEIRNE LAY Jr. and FRANK GILROY; Art Direction: WIARD IHMAN; Film Editor: FREDERICK Y. SMITH; Set Director: FRANK McKELVEY; Photography: JOE MacDONALD; Music Direction: ROGER WAGNER; Technical Advisor: JAMES T. GOTO

PT 109
Warner Bros., 1963
CAST: Lt. (jg) John F. Kennedy: CLIFF ROBERTSON; Ens. Leonard Thom: TY HARDIN; Cmdr. Ritchie: JAMES GREGORY; Ens. Barney Ross: ROBERT CULP; Lt. Alvin Cluster: GRANT WILLIAMS; "Bucky" Harris: ROBERT BLAKE
CREDITS: Director: LESLIE MARTINSON; Producer: BRYAN FOY; Screenplay: RICHARD BREEN; HOWARD SHEEHAN, VINCENT X. FLAHERTY; Original Story: ROBERT DONOVAN; Photography: ROBERT S. SURTEES; Film Editor: FOLMAR BLANGSTED; Art Direction: LEO K. KUTER; Set Direction: JOHN P. AUSTIN; Music Direction: WILLIAM LAVA and DAVID BUTTOLPH; Special Effects: RALPH WEBB

AMERICANIZATION OF EMILY
Metro-Goldwyn-Mayer, 1964
CAST: Lt. Cmdr. Charles E. Madison: JAMES GARNER; Emily Barham: JULIE ANDREWS; Adm. William Jessup: MELVYN DOUGLAS; Lt. Cmdr. "Bus" Cummings: JAMES COBURN; Mrs. Barham: JOYCE GRENFELL
CREDITS: Director: ARTHUR HILLER; Producer: MARTIN RANSOHOFF; Screenplay: PADDY CHAYEFSKY; Original Story: WILLIAM B. HUIE; Photography: PHILIP LATHROP; Film Editor: TOM MacADOO; Music Direction: JOHNNY MANDEL

ENSIGN PULVER
Warner Bros., 1964
CAST: Ens. Pulver: ROBERT WALKER; the Captain: BURL IVES; "Doc": WALTER MATTHAU; Bruno: TOMMY SANDS; Scotty: MILLIE PERKINS; Head Nurse: KAY MEDFORD. Other players are Larry Hagman, Gerald O'Loughlin, Sal Papa, Al Freeman Jr., James Farentino, James Coco, Don Dorell, Peter Marshall, Robert Matek, Diana Sands, and Joseph Marr
CREDITS: Director: JOSHUA LOGAN; Producer: JOSHUA LOGAN; Screenplay: JOSHUA LOGAN and PETER F. FEIBLEMAN; Photography: CHARLES LAWTON; Film Editor: WILLIAM REYNOLDS; Art Director: LEO K. KUTER; Music Direction: GEORGE DUHNING

McHALE'S NAVY
Universal International, 1964
Lt. Cmdr. Quinton McHale: ERNEST BORGNINE; Capt. Wallace Binghampton: JOE FLYNN; Ens. Charles Parker: TIM CONWAY; Lester Gruber: CARL BALLANTINE; George Christopher (Christy): GARY VINSON; Harrison "Tinker" Bell: BILLY SANDS; Virgil Edwards: EDSON STROLL. Other players are Gavin McLeod, John Wright, Yoshio Yoda, Bob Hastings, Claudine Longet, Jean Willes,

George Kennedy, Marcel Hillaire, Dale Ishimoto, John Mamo, Sandy Slvik.
CREDITS: Director: EDWARD J. MONTAGNE; Producer: EDWARD J. MONTAGNE; Screenplay: FRANK GILL JR. and C. CARLETON BROWN; Original Story: SI ROSE; Photography: WILLIAM MARGUILES; Film Editor: SAM E. WAXMAN; Art Direction: ALEXANDER GOLITZEN and RUSSELL KIMBAL; Set Directors: JOHN McCARTHY, JAMES S. REDD; Sound: WALDEN O. WATSON, EARL CRANE SR.; Music Direction: JERRY FIELDING

IN HARM'S WAY
Paramount, 1965
CAST: Rockwell Torrey: JOHN WAYNE; Cmdr. Paul Eddington: KIRK DOUGLAS; Lt. Maggie Haynes: PATRICIA NEAL; Lt. (J.G.) William McConnel: TOM TRYON; Bev McConnel: PAULA PRENTISS; Ens. Jeremiah Torrey: BRANDON de WILDE; Ens. Annalee Dorne: JILL HAWORTH; Adm. Broderick: DANA ANDREWS; Clayton Canfil: STANLEY HOLLOWAY; Cmdr. Powell: BURGESS MEREDITH; CINPAC Adm.: FRANCHOT TONE; Cmdr. Neal Gwynn: PATRICK O'NEAL; Cmdr. Burke: CARROLL O'CONNOR; CPO Culpepper: SLIM PICKENS; Liz Eddington: BARBARA BOUCHET; Air Force Major: HUGH O'BRIEN; CINPAC Adm.: HENRY FONDA; Ens. Griggs: JAMES MITCHUM; Col. Gregory: GEORGE KENNEDY. Other players are Tod Andrews, Larry Hagman, Stewart Moos, Soo Young, Dort Clark, and Phil Mattingly.
CREDITS: Director and Producer: OTTO PREMINGER; Screenplay: WENDELL MAYES; Original Story: JAMES BASSETT; Photography: FARCIOT EDOUART; Film Editor: GEORGE TOMASINI and HUGH FOWLER; Art Direction: AL ROELOFS; Set Direction: MORRIS HOFFMAN and RICHARD MANSFIELD; Special Effects: LAWRENCE BUTLER; Music Direction: JERRY GOLDSMITH; Technical Advisor: CAPTAIN COLIN J. MacKENZIE, USN

TORA! TORA! TORA!
Twentieth Century Fox, 1970
CAST: Adm. Kimmel: MARTIN BALSAM; Adm. Yamamoto: SOH YAMAMURA; Henry Stimson: JOSEPH COTTEN; Cmdr. Genda: TATSUYA MIHASHI; Lt. Col. Bratton: E.G. MARSHALL; Lt. Cmdr. Fuchida: TAKAHIRO TAMURA; Gen. Short: JASON ROBARDS; Adm. Halsey: JAMES WHITMORE; Adm. Nagumo: EIJARO TONO; Lt. Cmdr. Kramer: WESLEY ADDY; Adm. Nomura: SHOGO SHIMADA; Lt. Cmdr. Thomas: FRANK ALETTER; Prince Konoye: KOREYA SENDA; Frank Knox: LEON AMES; Gen. Marshall: KEITH ANDES; Adm. Stark: EDWARD ANDREWS; Lt. Kaminsly:

NEVILLE BRAND; Gen. Tojo: ASAO UCHIDA; Cordell Hull: GEORGE MACREADY; Maj. Landon: NORMAN ALDEN; Capt. Wilkinson: WALTER BROOKE; Lt. Welch: RICK COOPER; Doris Miller: ELVIN HAVARD; Miss Ray Cave: JUNE DAYTON; Cornelia: JEFF CONNELL; Col. French: RICHARD ERDMAN; Lt. Cmdr. Outerbridge: JERRY FOGEL; Kameto Kuroshima: SHUNICHI NAKAMURA; Lt. Taylor: CARL REINDL; Adm. Bellinger: EDMOND RYAN; Saburo Kurusu: HISAO TOAKE
CREDITS: Director: RICHARD FLEISCHER (U.S. Portions); TOSHIO MASUDA and KINJI FUKASUKU (Japanese Portions); Producer: ELMO WILLIAMS; Associate Producer: OTTO LANG, MASAYUKI TAKAGI, KEINOSUKE KUBO; Screenplay: LARRY FORRESTER; Original Story: GORDON PRANGE and LADISLAS FARAGO; Photography: CHARLES F. WHEELER (USA); SINASAKU HIMEDA, MASAMIECHI SATOH and OSAMI FURUYA; Film Editor: JAMES E. NEWCOM, PEMBROKE J. HERRING, INOUE CHIKAYA; Music Direction: JERRY GOLDSMITH; Art Direction: JACK MARTIN SMITH, YOSHIRO MURAKI, RICHARD DAY, and TAIZOH KAWASHIMA; Set Direction: WALTER M. SCOTT, NORMAN ROCKETT; Sound: JAMES CORCORAN, MURRAY SPIVAK, DOUG WILLIAMS, TED SODERBERG, HERMAN LEWIS; Special Effects: L.B. ABBOTT, ART CRUICKSHANK, SHIN WATARI; Aerial Photography: VISION PHOTOGRAPHY INC.; Technical Advisors: KAMEO SONOKAWA, KURNAOSHUKE ISODA, SHIZIO TAKADA, TSYYOSHI SAKA

MIDWAY
Universal Pictures, 1976
CAST: Matt Garth: CHARLTON HESTON; Adm. Chester W. Nimitz: HENRY FONDA; Capt. Maddox: JAMES COBURN; Adm. Spruance: GLENN FORD; Cmdr. Rochefort: HAL HOLBROOK; Adm. Yamamoto: TOSHIRO MIFUNE; Adm. William F. Halsey: ROBERT MITCHUM; Cmdr. Jessop: CLIFF ROBERTSON; Cmdr. Blake: ROBERT WAGNER. Other players are Robert Webber, Ed Nelson, James Shigeta, Christina Kokubo, Monte Markham, Biff McGuire, Kevin Dobson, Christopher George, Glenn Corbett, George Walcott, Edward Albert
CREDITS: Director: JACK SMIGHT; Producer: WALTER MIRISCH; Screenplay: DONALD S. SANFORD; Photography: HARRY STADLING Jr.; Film Editor: ROBERT SWINK, FRANK URIOSTE; Music Direction: JOHN WILLIAMS; Art Direction: WALTER TYLER; Set Direction: JOHN DWYER; Sound: ROBERT MARTIN, LEONARD PETERSON; Technical Advisor: Vice Adm. BERNARD M. STREAN, USN (Ret.)